David Milne

The Years and Eras of the Life of Christ

A demonstration of Gospel order and consistency for systematic teaching,

with two synopses showing other alternatives, untenable in Gospel

chronology and all the so-called discrepancies

David Milne

The Years and Eras of the Life of Christ
A demonstration of Gospel order and consistency for systematic teaching, with two synopses showing other alternatives, untenable in Gospel chronology and all the so-called discrepancies

ISBN/EAN: 9783337164140

Printed in Europe, USA, Canada, Australia, Japan

Cover: Foto ©Lupo / pixelio.de

More available books at **www.hansebooks.com**

THE YEARS AND ERAS

OF

THE LIFE OF CHRIST

*A DEMONSTRATION OF GOSPEL ORDER AND CONSISTENCY FOR
SYSTEMATIC TEACHING, WITH TWO SYNOPSES, SHOWING OTHER
ALTERNATIVES, UNTENABLE IN GOSPEL CHRONOLOGY·
AND ALL THE SO-CALLED DISCREPANCIES*

BY

DAVID MILNE, M.A.

AUTHOR OF

'A READABLE ENGLISH DICTIONARY.' (JOHN MURRAY) ETC.

LONDON

SIMPKIN, MARSHALL, HAMILTON, KENT & CO. LIMITED

EDINBURGH AND GLASGOW: JOHN MENZIES & CO.

ABERDEEN: A. & R. MILNE

1892

CONTENTS

THE YEARS AND ERAS

LIFE OF CHRIST.

——◆◆——

INTRODUCTION.

THE MAIN PECULIARITY of the following summary of the events of the Gospel History is the arrangement or classification of them. It will be shown, first, that at the natural[1] beginning of each solar year of the ministry of Jesus Christ a new era of it began, and that the close or consummation of each era is marked ; secondly, that each year is subdivided into four minor eras, ending with the four seasons or Jewish festivals, the Passover (Easter), Pentecost (Whitsunday), the Feast of Tabernacles about the beginning of October (the Jewish Tisri), and the Feast of Dedication, which began on the 25th of Kisleu (December) and ended on the 2nd of Thebet (January). It will be made evident that Jesus Christ attended these festivals successively in the successive years of His ministry—the Passover in the first year, Pentecost in the second, and the Feast of Tabernacles in the third ; that the fourth year commences with His departure from the Feast of Dedication (and with the Transfiguration) ; that each year bears the character of the feast which He attended in it ; and that an analogous development is discernible in the four minor eras of each year. The Jewish year and its festivals figured largely in the Old Testament economy ; and the developments thereby indicated reappear in the Gospel History. The didactic advantage of such a simple and natural grouping of the events, running through the entire public ministry of Jesus Christ, is obvious. Instead of appearing as a confusion of isolated incidents, very few of which are assigned in the mind to their proper connection, the

---

[1] Cæsar's original intention probably was to begin the year with the shortest day ; but as Jan. 1 B.C. 45 was the day of the new moon, he began it after the shortest days.

whole becomes a methodic study. Not only does classification lead the way to explanation ; but that which is learned methodically, with a view to system, is far more interesting, far more easily learned, and takes a much firmer hold on the mind, than incidents allowed to be unarranged and undigested in the mind.

THE CHARACTERISTIC FEATURES which distinguish the four Gospels, whether we take them from Irenæus or from an exponent of modern research, bear a striking analogy to the four stages of Gospel development. St. Mark's Gospel gives us a rapid but vivid and graphic 'outline of a considerable part of our Lord's history, forming the historical framework of the three Synoptic Gospels ; ' it wants the 'expanded and attractive narratives ' of the other Evangelists and 'all the longer discourses except that about the Second Advent ; ' it does not contain the Lord's Prayer, and has only four Parables. It gives a bird's or an eagle's eye view of the subject, running concisely over it (σύντομον καὶ παρατρέχουσαν), as Irenæus describes it (iii. 11, 8), and begins by connecting itself with the dispensation by Isaiah and other Hebrew Prophets, which preceded. St. Matthew, again, abounds in discourses of 'great literary power, theological interest, and spiritual value.' The Sermon on the Mount, which is its 'chief glory,' consists entirely of plain preceptive teaching, but the parable of the Unmerciful Servant and Christ's identification of Himself with His needy and destitute servants 'have done even more to humanise the age in which we live.' His Gospel presents Him as a King adored by the Magi ; but His Kingdom is within men ; Jesus is throughout the Man, meek and lowly-minded (Iren. iii. 11, 8), giving *rest* to those who *learn* of Him (Matt. xi. 29). St. Luke's object, as stated in his preface, was to give to those already catechetically instructed the certainty of fuller or more perfect knowledge (ἵνα ἐπιγνῷς τὴν ἀσφάλειαν). It was also the desire of St. Paul, whom St. Luke accompanied, that the Christians should attain this more perfect knowledge (ἐπίγνωσις) of the mystery of God (Col. ii. 2). St. Luke's Gospel abounds 'in fascinating narratives, parables, and parabolic stories.' The peculiar section of it (ix. 51–xviii. 14) is rich in parabolic teaching of its own ; 'its crowning glory is the Parable of the Prodigal Son,' because of whose finding the fatted calf was killed (Iren. iii. 2. 8). This sacrificial aspect of the Gospel, characterising ' the Pauline teaching so prominent in it,' appears also in the priestly details of the first chapters. As the Gospel of the Gentiles, it exhibits a 'cosmopolitan spirit.' St. John's Gospel begins with a declaration that the Word of God was made flesh and dwelt among us ; it exhibits Jesus Christ as the Son of God, one with the Father (x. 30, 36).

as the Lion of the tribe of Judah, 'in everything a conqueror, especially reigning from the cross (xvi. 33). Even in its miracles it teems with teaching full of spiritual power and sublimity.'[1]

THE ORDER OF THE THREE LAST EVANGELISTS (Mark, Luke, and John) is proved to be in full chronological consistency, and is followed in this summary without any material deviation. It will be shown that St. Luke[2] does not transpose Christ's visit to Nazareth or the call of the four fishermen, but that he is relating different incidents, which fit into different places of the history; that the true chronological position of the Mission of the Seventy has been misunderstood by not attending to a very simple rule of historical narration; and that in consequence of this misunderstanding there is a want of harmony among the harmonists. It is now generally admitted that St. Matthew's order is not exactly chronological, but sometimes modified for didactic purposes. Thus he groups together the miracles, postponing the healing of Peter's wife's mother and anticipating the cure of the two demoniacs of Gerasa or Gadara.

[1] The words marked in this paragraph as quotations are cited from a small book on the Composition of the Gospels by the Rev. A. Wright, M.A. (Macmillan, 1890). Mr. Wright compares the law of progress in Revelation, ' or the development proved by a comparison of Mark with Matthew and Luke, and these again with John's personal recollections, to the change from childhood through youth to manhood.' Perhaps this is too strong a statement; and we certainly need not follow Mr. Wright in his conjecture that the first three stages were successive developments, proceeding from a common centre, Mark representing the first cycle, Matthew the first and second cycles, and Luke the first, second, and third cycles. Their similarities may be accounted for by the long intimate intercourse between Peter, who had Mark for his interpreter, Matthew, and Luke, or Luke's authorities. According to the late Bishop Lightfoot, the best-founded knowledge of the composition of the Gospels will be obtained by a careful study of Irenæus and his contemporaries, and of the grounds they had for attributing the Gospels to those whose names they bear. Irenæus and the early Christians believed that the four aspects of the Gospel have a world-wide significance, and are due to divine pre-arrangement. They identified these aspects with the four Faces of the Cherubim—the Eagle, the Man, the Ox, and the Lion. St. John mentions these Faces in the reverse order (Rev. iv. 7); and this is accounted for at the end of this treatise. In the dispensation by Moses there are also indications of a four-fold progress, similar to that of Gospel developments.

[2] St. Luke professes to write 'in order' (Luke i. 3); but many harmonists think that he means doctrinal, not chronological order. McClellan draws up a detailed conspectus exhibiting St. Luke's Gospel in the form of a long doctrinal discourse, with main headings, minor divisions and sub-divisions (*Four Gospels*, pp. 425–438). He criticises the previous attempts of Ebrard, Oosterzee, and Westcott, and finds their connections, analogies, and titles fanciful or unsatisfactory. His own will scarcely commend itself.

THE EARLY GOSPEL HISTORY AND CONNECTED EVENTS.

PALESTINE had, for some time before the commencement of the Christian era, become a dependency of Rome. Its real independence had come to an end when the rival claims of the two Asmonean or Maccabean princes, the warlike Aristobulus and the weak Hyrcanus, had been decided by Pompey in favour of Hyrcanus, supported as he was by Herod's cunning father, the Idumean Antipater. Pompey took Jerusalem on the Day of Atonement (about October 1), in the year of Rome (A.U.C.) 691, or B.C. 63,[1] the famous year of Cicero's consulship (Jos. 'Ant.' xiv. 4, 3). After twenty-two years, during which the ambitious Antipater had appointed his sons, Phasael to be governor of Jerusalem, and Herod, a stern and vigorous prince, to be governor of Galilee, the Parthians invaded Syria and Asia Minor. By their means Antigonus, the son of Aristobulus, got possession of Jerusalem. This was shortly after Pentecost. Herod, escaping in time from Jerusalem, visited Arabia and Egypt, but made haste to get to Rome in spite of very stormy weather ($\chi\epsilon\iota\mu\hat{\omega}\nu\sigma$). Here he arrived shortly after the reconciliation of Antony and Augustus by the treaty of Brundisium. By Antony's help Herod obtained a decree of the Senate, appointing him king of Judea and declaring Antigonus to be an enemy of Rome. This was towards the close of the year A.U.C. 714.[2] Herod stayed only seven days at Rome. Antigonus, who had begun to reign shortly after Pentecost A.U.C. 711, reigned for three years and three months ('Ant.' xx. 10); Herod and the Roman general Sosius then took Jerusalem again on the Day of Atonement A.U.C. 717 (Jos. 'Ant.' xiv. 16, 4); and soon after, at the instigation of Herod, his Maccabean rival Antigonus was put to death. Herod's accession followed in A.U.C. 717, for the battle of Actium, fought in Sept.

---

[1] The year 1 of the Christian era corresponds with the year of Rome 754. Hence B.C. 63 corresponds with A.U.C. 754 − 63, or 691 ; but A.D. 63 with A.U.C. 753 + 63, or 816.

[2] Josephus (*Ant.* xiv. 14, 5) says that Herod was appointed king in the consulship of C. Asinius Pollio and Cn. Domitius Calvinus (ii.), and in the 184th Olympiad ; but as this Olympiad ended at midsummer 714 A.U.C., Josephus must have mixed the Roman way of reckoning years with the Greek ; and thus reckoned the whole of A.U.C. 714 as belonging to the 184th Olympiad. But by no reckoning can the year A.U.C. 715 be included in the 184th Olympiad ; and Caspari (p. 20), in attempting to do so, has by mistake substituted the years of the 185th for those of the 184th Olympiad.

A.U.C. 723 or B.C. 31, was in the seventh year after it (Jos. 'Ant.'
xv. 5, 2). By his victory, Augustus became sole Emperor.
THE BIRTH OF CHRIST preceded the death of Herod by at
least some months, and we can approximately determine the date
of Herod's death. Josephus tells us ('Ant.' xvii. 8, 1 ; 'Wars,' i. 33,
8) that Herod reigned thirty-seven years after his nomination by
the Romans and thirty-four years after he got rid of Antigonus ;
but the difficulty is to decide how Josephus reckoned such num-
bers. The Jewish year began with the first of Nisan (April), and
the odd months of a king's reign before his first Nisan were
reckoned his first year ; the months following this Nisan were
reckoned his second year ; and if there were any months, or even
days, after the king's last Nisan 1, they were also counted as a
year. This mode of reckoning was not confined to kings' reigns
or to years.[1] It must have been in this way that Josephus
reckoned twenty-seven years between the capture of Jerusalem
by Pompey, A.U.C. 691, and its capture by Herod and Sosius,
A.U.C. 717. Both captures took place on the Day of Atonement,
so that there were exactly twenty-six years between them ; but in
all probability Josephus reckoned the odd months from the first
capture to Nisan 1 as one year, and the odd months from Nisan 1
to the second capture as another (the twenty-seventh) year.
Again, Josephus reckons 107 years from Herod's accession in
A.U.C. 717 to the destruction of the Temple by the Romans in
August A.U.C. 823, although there were really not 106 complete
years. Reckoning in this way, we should conclude that Herod
died sometime between Nisan 1, A.U.C. 750, and Nisan 1, A.U.C. 751.
We know also from Josephus ('Ant.' xvii. 6, 4 ; 9, 3 ; 'Wars,' ii. 1, 3)
that Herod died not long after an eclipse of the moon, and shortly
before the Passover. There was a partial eclipse of the moon in
A.U.C. 750, on the night between March 12 and 13,[2] and this

---

[1] In exactly the same way Jesus Christ is said eight times in the Gospels
and once in St. Paul's Epistles to rise or have risen from the dead on the
third day, it being the invariable custom to call the next day but one the third
day, reckoning the hours preceding sunset as the first day. Not only so, but
Christ is said to have risen after three days (Matt. xxvii. 63, explained in
next verse; Mark viii. 31 ; cp. Gen. xlii. 17, 18; 2 Chron. x. 5, 12) ; and
when Jesus Christ Himself referred to the interment of Jonah for three days
and three nights in the whale's belly, He predicted that He would be the same
time in the grave. There may have been, as Lightfoot suggested, a Hebrew
(ōnah) or Aramaic equivalent of the one Greek word nychthemeron, a night
and a day ; but, whether or not, Jesus only followed a common way of
speaking, and in so doing adopted the words in Jonah.

[2] There were also two total eclipses of the moon in A.U.C. 749—one in
March, and the other in September ; no eclipse in A.U.C. 751 and 752, but
a total eclipse on January 10, A.U.C. 753.

corresponds best with other data. If we allow three weeks for the intervening events during Herod's illness, and suppose that he died in the first week of April, there would only be the objection that Josephus thus counted a few days in the beginning of Nisan as a whole year. The Talmudists certainly reckoned kings' reigns in this way. The alternative is to suppose that the intervening events—the king's visit to the warm baths of Callirrhoë, &c. —were extended over several months, that he died about August or September, A.U.C. 750, and that the Passover referred to was that of A.U.C. 751. Herod was succeeded in Judea, Samaria, and Idumea by his son Archelaus, in Perea and Galilee by his son Herod Antipas, and in the northern parts of ancient Bashan by Philip the Tetrarch. Archelaus was banished to Vienne in A.U C. 759 (Dion Cassius), which is doubtfully called by Josephus both the ninth ('Wars,' ii. 7, 3) and the tenth year ('Ant.'xvii. 13, 2) of his government; and his provinces were then governed by a Roman procurator, who resided mostly at Cæsarea. Philip the Tetrarch died in the twentieth year of Tiberius, that is, in the 787th year of Rome, after he had been tetrarch for thirty-seven years ('Ant.' xviii. 4, 6). The inference from these data is that Herod died about the beginning of April A U.C. 750; and reckoning back three months for the intervening events, we have every reason to believe that Jesus Christ was born about or shortly before the commencement of A.U.C. 750—that is, four years before the era assigned by Dionysius Exiguus in the sixth century.

THE DAY OF CHRIST'S NATIVITY is approximately determined. The tradition both of the Eastern and Western Churches has uniformly handed down January 6, the Feast of Epiphany (Manifestation), as the day of Christ's baptism; and there is evidence that the anniversary of His birth was kept on the same day with it. Epiphanius tells us expressly that the Egyptians celebrated our Lord's birth on the 11th of their month Tybi, which corresponds to January 6 (Wieseler, 'E. T.,' p. 115, note 3). The inconvenience of celebrating the birth and baptism on the same day, the one at Bethlehem and the other at the Jordan, was one reason for altering the anniversary of Christ's birth to December 25. Chrysostom, writing in A.D. 387 concerning the day of the Nativity, gives us to understand that until ten years previous to his writing —that is, up to A.D. 377—the Eastern Churches had observed the anniversary of Christ's nativity on the same day as they commemorated His baptism—namely, on January 6; but that, in deference to the superior means of knowing which the Romans had in the census lists, &c., they had already come to keep a separate anniversary for Christ's birth—namely December 25 (see

McClellan's 'Four Gospels,' p. 407). There is no reason to depart from the general tradition of the Church that Jesus was baptised on January 6 ; and St. Luke tells us that He was then about thirty years old. The objection that at the season of Christmas, or January 6, the shepherds of Bethlehem would not be at night in the open air (ἀγραυλοῦντες) admits of explanation. First, the shepherds were not ordinary shepherds, but keepers or purveyors of animals for the Temple sacrifices. They had a place near Bethlehem, called Migdal Eder, 'the Tower of the Flock ;' and there was a belief that the advent of the Messiah would be proclaimed from it (Edersheim's 'Life of Christ,' vol. i. p. 186). Secondly, there is no reason to disbelieve that their flocks would be in the fields at this season. The Jewish Mishnah speaks of them as being in the field thirty days before the Passover ; and the rainfall in February is greater than at Christmas, which in Palestine is sometimes one of the loveliest periods in the year (Andrews, new edit. pp. 15–18 ; Edersheim, i. p. 87). Besides this, when the spring rains cease in April, the whole country soon becomes dry and barren, so that, according to the traveller Barclay ('City of the Great King,' p. 423), the nomad Arabs have in June to move northward with their flocks. Another argument is based on what we know of the course of Abijah, to which Zacharias, the father of John the Baptist, belonged. It was the eighth of twenty-four courses, each of which ministered in turn for one week. Now we learn from the Talmud that on the day of the destruction of the Temple, the 9th or 10th of Ab (August) A.U.C. 823, the first course, that of Jehoiarib, had just entered upon their ministry. Reckoning backwards, it has been calculated (e.g. by Wieseler, Greswell, Browne, Caspari, &c.) that the course of Abijah was in office during the first week of October A.U.C. 748. This, therefore, was the time of the angel's appearance to Zacharias ; and the inference from this in connection with Luke i. 26 and 36 is that the ecclesiastical date of the Annunciation to Mary—that is Lady Day, or March 25—is approximately correct, and, therefore, that Jesus Christ was born on or about December 25 A.U.C. 749.[1]

THE DECREE OF CÆSAR AUGUSTUS that there should be a general census or enrolment, as the word (apographé) is translated in the Revised Version of Luke ii. 1, 2, is quite in harmony with what we know of Augustus from other than Biblical sources.

---

[1] December 25 A.U.C. 749, is the date of Christ's birth assigned by Petavius, Usher, Browne (Ordo Seculorum), Andrews, McClellan, Edersheim, Lichtenstein, and the Christian Church, while Bengel, Wieseler, Greswell, Thomson, and Ellicott prefer an early date in A.U.C. 750.

Tacitus tells us that he wrote 'out with his own hand a summary of statistics of the whole empire' ('Annals,' 2, 11 ; Suet. 'Aug.' 28). The enrolment or registration was with a view to taxation, and seems to have been first of persons (Luke ii. 2) and, secondly, of persons and property (Acts v. 37 ; Jos. 'Ant.' xvii. 13, 5). The poll-tax, called *census* (κῆνσος) in the New Testament (Matt. xvii. 25 ; Mark xii. 14), was a Roman denarius (or attic drachma), valued by the revisers at 8½*d*. (Matt. xviii. 28), but put for a day's wages (Matt. xx. 9). We know both from St. Luke (Acts v. 37) and from Josephus ('Ant.' xviii. 1, 1) that this registration was exceedingly distasteful to the Jews, and provoked insurrection. St. Luke tells us that 'it was first made when Cyrenius was governor of Syria ;' but the word (ἐγένετο) translated 'made' has also the sense of 'accomplished,' 'effected,' or 'carried out,' in St. Luke's writings (Acts xi. 28). Josephus tells us that Cyrenius was appointed governor (legate) of Syria after the banishment of Archelaus, that is, nine or ten years after Christ's birth, to settle the affairs of Archelaus and take an account of the people's effects. But Dr. A. W. Zumpt, of Berlin, has made it highly probable that Cyrenius (P. Sulpicius Quirinius) also succeeded Quintilius Varus as the governor of Syria about the middle of A.U.C. 750, and held the office then for three years and a half. He may even have previously held some subordinate office as procurator or fiscal president, like Pilate and Felix, who were also called governors, and in this capacity he may have carried out the first registration or census ; but it is not unlikely that so unpopular a measure was delayed, perhaps by the troubles connected with Herod's last illness and death, and that it was not 'carried into effect' till the first or even the second government of Cyrenius as legate. It was, no doubt, to make it less distasteful that the Jews were first registered according to their ideas of kindred and country.

THE VISIT OF THE MAGI, or Wise Men of the East, was occasioned by the appearance of a remarkable star in the East, which they witnessed about two years previous to their visit (Matt. ii. 16). Now it is astronomically certain that there was a brilliant conjunction of the planets Jupiter and Saturn in A.U.C. 747, that this conjunction, which was in the constellation Pisces, occurred three times during this year, and in next spring with Mars, and must have been very conspicuous in the East. There was also a Jewish tradition that such a conjunction occurred in the constellation Pisces before the birth of Moses; and, accordingly, the Jewish commentator Abarbanel, writing in the fifteenth century, and before Kepler calculated this conjunction, laid it down that such a conjunction in Pisces would herald the advent of the Messiah (Wieseler, p. 59). Kepler saw similar conjunctions of these planets in Dec. 1603, and spring 1604. Next autumn a brilliant star appeared near them. Other evanescent stars have, however, been seen by Tycho Brahe and others to come into view and slowly to disappear, as if into distant space ; and we do not know how much about the star of Bethlehem was miraculous. We do not, therefore, have sufficient data to decide what this star was. According to Justin Martyr (' Dial.' 78), the voice from Ramah, spoken of by Jeremiah the prophet (Jer. xxxi. 15 ; Matt. ii. 17, 18), was this visit of the Magi ; for he says that, even in his time there was a place in Arabia called Ramah (cp. Gen. x. 7). The lamentation and weeping did not constitute the voice, but followed it ; and Rachel is represented as weeping for her children, because she was buried at or near Bethlehem.

THE RETURN OF THE CHILD JESUS FROM EGYPT followed the death of Herod. As Herod died shortly before the Passover, the child Jesus may have been called out of Egypt about the time of the Passover, as Israel, the type of God's Son, was called out of Egypt at the time of the Passover (Hosea xi. 1 ; Matt. ii. 15). The family returned to Nazareth. The name which the Jews would give to Jesus would therefore be *Nozri*—that is, Nazarene— and this word sums up their idea of the divinely appointed Branch, called *Nezer* by Isaiah (xi. 1), and *Zemach* by Jeremiah (xxiii. 5; xxxiii. 15) and Zechariah (iii. 8). Their liturgy spoke of the Branch of David speedily to 'shoot forth,' and blessed Jehovah, who causes to ' branch forth ' the horn of salvation (15th Eulogy).

AT THE AGE OF TWELVE the boy Jesus attended the Passover with His parents. 'Only on two days of the Passover,' says Dr. Edersheim (i. 246), 'was personal attendance necessary.' On the first day the Paschal lamb was eaten at night, and, after day came, the festive sacrifices of the feast (Chag) or festivity (Chagigah), were offered and eaten. The second day was a high day, because on it the people assembled in holy convocation before the Lord in the Temple, and an omer of the flour of the first reaped barley was waved before the Lord. After this 'there was nothing of special interest to detain the pilgrims,' and Joseph and Mary probably availed themselves of the permission to go home. But during the rest of the Passover week ' it was usual for the members of the Temple Sanhedrim to come out upon the terrace of the Temple and to teach' (p. 247). Among these doctors the parents of Jesus found Him ' both hearing them and asking them questions,' and astonishing them by His understanding and ·discernment. Of these doctors the bulk of the Rabbinist or Pharisaic

section belonged to the school of Hillel (like Gamaliel); their
ideal kingdom was that of a divinely-instituted rule of the Rabbis;
they were inclined to keep aloof from the ignorant people who
knew not the law (John vii. 49). The school of Shammai, again,
was intensely national or Zealot. Their maxim, *Mi Camochah
Baalim Jehovah* (Who is like thee among the gods, Jehovah?)
made with its initials the word *Maccabee*, and showed them to be
opposed to all lordship except that of Jehovah. The Boethians,
whom we may identify with the Herodians, united moderate
Pharisaic principles with political attachment to the reigning
family. They were named from Boethus, an Alexandrian priest,
whose son Joazar Herod on his death-bed had made high priest.
Joazar, however, had taken the popular part against Archelaus,
and, with a view to conciliate the Romans, had persuaded the
Jews to submit to the taxing of Cyrenius. But, in spite of this
assistance, Cyrenius, legate of the province of Syria, in which
Judea was now incorporated, distrusted Joazar, and appointed
Annas, or Ananus, high priest in his place. Afterwards the office
was mostly held by Annas himself, or members of his family, and
after Christ's death Annas continued to be the chief director in
the counsels of the Sanhedrim. Annas and his family were
Sadducees, serving the Roman government as its instruments, and
allowing the Pharisees to carry out their strict religious formali-
ties, although they disbelieved in much of them; they were
somewhat sceptical, but, like Caiaphas, guided by expediency
(John xviii. 14). Coponius, the first Roman procurator of Judea,
now held office under Cyrenius, legate of Syria.

FOR EIGHTEEN YEARS AFTER THIS PASSOVER Jesus lived at
Nazareth, continuing subject to His parents, working at Joseph's
occupation as a carpenter (Mark vi. 3), and growing in wisdom
and in favour with God and man.

JOHN THE BAPTIST BEGAN HIS MINISTRY in the fifteenth
year of the hegemony or rule of Tiberius Cæsar (Luke iii. 1).
St. Luke, however, must have reckoned this rule to commence
with the appointment of Tiberius in January 765, A.U.C., to
administer the provinces as the colleague of Augustus, and as
having equal authority (*æquum jus*) with him. Augustus died on
March 19, A.U.C. 767, or A.D. 14. Pontius Pilate had entered
upon his office shortly before John's ministry began, for Pilate
was ten full years governor of Judea, and left very shortly before
the death of Tiberius, which took place on March 16, A.U.C. 790,
or A.D. 37 (Jos. 'Ant.' xviii. 4, 2). Pilate, therefore, entered on his
office in the early summer of A.U.C. 779, and John must have
entered on his office about October 1, A.U.C. 779, at the commencement of what Wieseler shows to have been a Sabbatical

year ; that is, if John appeared about October 1, some months had intervened after Pilate's arrival, and some months again intervened· before the baptism of Jesus. John was the last of the prophets (Matt. xi. 13), and came to close the dispensation by them. When the Jews asked why he baptised, seeing he was neither Elijah, nor the Messiah, nor that prophet, they probably had in their minds the words of Ezekiel (xxxvi. 25-27): 'I also will sprinkle clean water upon you, and ye shall be clean . . . a new heart will I give you,' &c. Though John did not claim this consummation for his baptism, yet his baptism was the highest level to which the previous dispensational elements attained ; it was related to them as the perfect cleansing spoken of by Ezekiel was to the initiatory stages of Christianity, and there may therefore be some significance in the season when John commenced his ministry, when compared with what occurred afterwards at this season. The scene of John's labours was the neighbourhood of the Jordan, and the wilderness of Judea. Now this might be somewhere not far north from the mouth of the Jordan ; or it might be in Judea beyond Jordan, as St. Matthew calls it (Matt. xix. 1)—that is, in Northern Perea or Bashan. There was also a wilderness of Judea in the far south, but this was not the wilderness of John's baptism, as it was not beside the Jordan.

Synoptical Table of Early Gospel History.

Christ's Birth and Mission heralded

	Matt.	Mark	Luke	John
St. Matthew begins his Gospel with the Hebrew Book of Generation,[1] or pedigree of Jesus Christ as the son and heir of David and Abraham.	i. 1–17			
St. Mark connects the beginning of the Gospel of Jesus Christ with the end of Hebrew line of prophets in John the Baptist's mission.		i. 1		
St. Luke states in his preface that his history was written for the fuller instruction of catechumens, and extends Christ's genealogy[2] to Adam.			i. 1–4 iii. 23–38	

[1] To make up St. Matthew's second list of fourteen generations reckon Jechonias I. as Jehoiakim, and Jechonias II. as Jehoiachin. The three names have all the same meaning in Hebrew, namely, 'whom God hath established.' Ahaziah, Joash, Amaziah, descendants of Athaliah, are omitted.

[2] The genitive relation translated 'son of' in St. Luke's genealogy admits of other meanings, as 'father,' 'brother,' &c., and might mean 'reputed son

	Matt.	Mark	Luke	John
St. John begins his Gospel by setting forth Jesus Christ as God's Word, by whom all things were made, who became man to reveal the Father.				i. 1–14
The birth of John was announced beforehand by an angel to Zacharias, and the birth of Jesus to the Virgin Mary, whose hymn is called the *Magnificat*.			i. 5–25 / i. 26–56	
Joseph was informed in a dream that Christ's birth was of the Holy Spirit.	i. 18–25			
On the birth of John, Zacharias blessed the Lord in the hymn called *Benedictus*.			i. 57–80	
Jesus Christ was born at Bethlehem about December 25, A.U.C. 749, B.C. 4.			ii. 1–7	
An epiphany (manifestation of God's glory), with angels singing *Gloria in Excelsis*, proclaimed this to shepherds, keeping animals for Temple sacrifices.			ii. 8–20	
On the eighth day, the child was circumcised ; and, forty days after His birth, He was presented in the Temple, when Simeon declared His mission.			ii. 21–40	
Also Wise Men, guided by a star, came from the East to worship Him as King ; but Herod, hearing from them of His birth, killed all the babes in Bethlehem.	ii. 1–12 / ii. 13–18			
Joseph and Mary, after fleeing to Egypt, brought the child to Nazareth.	ii. 19–23			
At the age of twelve, the boy Jesus went to the Passover with His parents.			ii. 41–50	
During nearly eighteen years Jesus worked as a carpenter, growing in wisdom.		vi. 3	ii. 51, 52	
About Midsummer or October, A.D. 26, John the Baptist began his public ministry.	iii. 1–12	i. 2–8	iii. 1–18	

(Luke iii. 23), or 'son-in-law.' Thus, if Joseph was the son-in-law of Heli, we have in St. Luke the genealogy of the mother of Jesus. So Salathiel, or Shealtiel, was the son of Jehoiachin (Matt. i. 12) and probably son-in-law of Neri (Luke iii. 27). If we adopt the Revised Text of Luke iii. 23, and read ὢν υἱός, ὡς ἐνομίζετο Ἰωσήφ, τοῦ Ἡλί, perhaps we should rather translate, ' being the son, as Joseph was reputed, of Heli,' that is, being the grandson of Heli, as Joseph was reputed to be his son (see Andrews).

THE FOUR YEARS OF CHRIST'S MINISTRY.

THERE WERE FOUR PASSOVER SEASONS during the public ministry of Jesus Christ. This was early pointed out by Irenæus (ii. 32, 3), who in reckoning them made also the important statement that, during the last of them, Jesus 'both ate the Passover and suffered on the following day.' The points at issue with those who would reckon three instead of four such seasons or years may be briefly indicated. All the three Synoptists (Matthew, Mark, and Luke) relate the plucking of the ears of corn by the disciples and place it at some interval of time, more or less, before that Passover, near the time of which the Five Thousand were fed. Now, if the Passover referred to was that of the same year in which the ears were plucked, the ministry of Jesus Christ would cover one year less than it would cover if the feeding of the Five Thousand was at the Passover of the following year. But ripe ears of corn could not be had, even in the early spots of Palestine, before the beginning of Nisan (April) ; and the Passover was sacrificed on the 14th of Nisan. If therefore the Passover when the Five Thousand were fed was that of the same year when the ears were plucked, then we should have to crowd into the . space of something like ten days, or at most a fortnight, all the intervening events mentioned by St. Mark and St. Luke—the Great Sermon, several great miracles, perhaps two circuits, Boat Parables, the visit to Gergesa (Gerasa), the Mission and return of the apostles, &c.[1] We have the alternative of following the order of St. Matthew, who places the Sermon on the Mount, the visit to Gerasa, and the Mission of the Apostles before the plucking of the ears of corn. But, as has been said, St. Matthew's order seems to be modified by didactic considerations ; and when the order of two Evangelists (Mark and Luke) coincides, it must be considered to be chronological, for two writers following independent lines of didactic order would probably not so agree with one another. This consideration also sets aside the conclusions of some others, who, rather than admit this year or Passover season, regard the order of details in all the three Synoptists as not chronological but determined by didactic combinations, although they admit

[1] Wieseler, in his Synopsis of the Four Gospels (pp. 164, 285), attempts to do this ! In this way he limits the mission of the apostles to one day !

B

certain chronological limits within which the incidents occurred.[1] But this supposition is needless, for why should not the ministry of Jesus Christ extend to four years, especially if the second-first day, mentioned by St. Luke (vi. 1) as being the Sabbath on which the ears of corn were plucked, was the *second* day of the Passover required and the *first* day of counting the weeks to Pentecost?

THE FIRST YEAR OF CHRIST'S MINISTRY.
A.D. 27.

Significant Manifestations without other Recorded Teaching.

This year (A.D. 27) begins with the baptism of Jesus by John on or about January 6; and ends, as we shall show, with Christ's declaring Himself at Nazareth to be the fulfilment of Messianic prophecy, before His settlement at Capernaum. Whatever other things Jesus may have this year taught, the Gospels only record certain significant manifestations of Himself and announcements of the coming Spirit and true worship, without explanations or specific moral directions. The character of the first year's ministry was shown at the Passover which Jesus attended this year. At the Passover He predicted His own death and resurrection, thus giving a sign of a New Temple ; and of these two fundamental facts the Pauline theology is an exposition. The discourse with Nicodemus is merely a declaration of the coming of the Holy Spirit consequent on the lifting up of the Son of Man ; and the baptising through the disciples was an outward and visible sign of what was to be fulfilled in the progress of Christianity.

AT HIS BAPTISM Jesus was 'about thirty years of age, beginning' (Luke iii. 23), that is, entering upon the canonical age of the priesthood (Num. iv. 3, 23) and the age when the typical King David began to reign (2 Sam: v. 4). Every priest was consecrated to his office by baptism and by anointing with oil (Lev. viii. 6, 12). Now this consecration was fulfilled in the case of Jesus by the baptism of John and by the descent upon Him of the Holy Spirit, typified by the oil of consecration.

AT HIS FIRST POST-BAPTISMAL PASSOVER, Jesus cleansed the Temple courts ; and, in answer to the question of the Jews, ' What sign showest thou, seeing that thou doest these things?' Jesus referred to His own death and resurrection, and indicated that He would thereby supersede the Temple service and raise up a new and cleansed Temple. But the Jews thought that He

[1] Caspari (*Introduction*, p. 152) and Edersheim (*Life of Christ*, vol. ii. pp. 51-55), by omitting this Passover season, come to this conclusion:

spoke of rebuilding Herod's Temple, which, with its courts, had been already forty-six years in building.[1]

THE DISCOURSE WITH NICODEMUS took place after the miracles which Jesus did at the Passover had become well known (John ii. 23 ; iii. 2). The visit, therefore, could not have taken place till the end of the Passover ; and it may have occurred some weeks later, not improbably at the following Pentecost. The Passover was the season of Christ's death and resurrection ; and accordingly it was at the Passover that Christ first prominently announced these events. So Pentecost was the season when the disciples were directed to await the promised Spirit ; and as the day was thus of importance, it is not improbable that Christ first prominently announced to Nicodemus on the day of Pentecost the coming of this Spirit. The Spirit came at Pentecost with the sound of a rushing mighty wind ; and so, in the conversation with Nicodemus, Jesus compares the coming of the Spirit to the wind. It is sufficient, however, to assign this conversation generally to the period between the Passover and Pentecost, or to the time of the Pentecostal harvest.

THE BAPTISING BY JESUS MEDIATELY through His disciples took place in some country district of Judea, and 'after these things,' that is, after the discourse with Nicodemus. This baptising was peculiar work; and being begun would probably continue some time. As the discourse with Nicodemus connects itself in its substance with the feast of Pentecost, so by this putting His disciples 'before His face' to baptise in His name, we are reminded of what Jesus afterwards said at the Feast of Tabernacles (John vii. 38, 39), namely, that those who believed in Him would receive from Him living water, and dispense it to others. This idea of veiled and mediated teaching was indicated by Isaiah (xl. 10 ; lxii. 11) when he speaks of the coming of the Lord and His putting 'His work (recompense) before His face.' The baptism of the Word (λογικὸς βαπτισμός), as Clement of Alexandria calls it ('Pæd.' i. 6), was a covert (parabolic) way of presenting

---

[1] Herod began to build the Temple in the 18th year of his reign (Jos. *Ant.* xv. 11, 1). Reckoning from A.U.C. 717, we should have the proper date of Christ's first post-baptismal Passover, for 717 + 17 + 46 = 780 A.U.C. We have here a confirmation of the date of Christ's birth, A.U.C. 750: but unfortunately another account is given in Josephus, *Wars*, i. 21, 1, where Herod is said to have rebuilt the Temple in his 15th year. , Caspari reckons the 15th year from the death of Antigonus, and the 18th year from Herod's nomination by the Romans : and, as this method gives too early a date for the other data, he concludes that somewhere Josephus miscounted two years. It is more likely that some blundering scribe changed the number (Wieseler, p. 52, note).

Himself, as Israel (God's Son) appeared under a covering (of booths) at the Feast of Tabernacles. ' All men came to Him ' to be so baptised (John iii. 26). Accordingly we are warranted in connecting this baptising by Jesus through His disciples with the mediated provision He made for the multitudes in His third year's ministry and with the Feast of Tabernacles, as in all probability Jesus and His disciples were baptising about the season of this feast, in the beginning of October.

THE JOURNEY OF JESUS THROUGH SAMARIA to Galilee, and His interview with the woman at the well of Sychar, took place four months before the harvest. When the people of Sychar were coming out of their city to Him, Jesus pointed them out to His disciples as the beginning of the harvest of the world which they were to reap. ' Say ye not,' said He to them, ' it is *yet* four months and then cometh the harvest? Behold . . . the fields are white to harvest already ' (John iv. 35). Now this was not a proverbial expression, for, first, no such proverb is anywhere mentioned or alluded to ; and, secondly, if it had been a proverbial expression, it would have been, ' Are there not four months *after seed-time*, and then cometh the harvest?' ; and, thirdly, in Palestine, there are six months between the seed-time and the harvest. Dr. Edersheim (vol. i. 419, 420) supposes that Jesus pointed to the fields literally ripe for harvest, and admonished His disciples at the same time that it was a mistake to say in their hearts that the Messianic kingdom or spiritual harvest of the world was still months distant ; that sowing and harvesting in the spiritual world are often commingled. But He bade them not disconnect Christian sowing from reaping the old preparation, as at the *close* of the next year He showed the ideal Scribe's things new and old. The Jewish harvest legally began on the second day of the Passover, after the first *omer* (translated *sheaf*) of the barley, cut down in a sheltered valley leading down to the tropical Ghôr, had been threshed, ground, and presented in the Temple. To make the Passover correspond with the beginning of harvest and rectify the calendar, an additional Adar (March), called Veadar, was added every third year. Reckoning back four months from the Passover, we conclude that Jesus passed through Samaria before the middle of December.[1] There remained at least two weeks of the year, during which Jesus visited Cana and began to teach in the synagogues of Galilee.

[1] Wieseler, Robinson, Ellicott, Meyer, Hengstenberg, Godet, Andrews, and others understand that Jesus went through Samaria four months before the harvest. McClellan, who places this journey at the end of May, supposes that the first circuit in Galilee occupied nine or ten months of the time till the plucking of the ears of corn ! So Greswell.

THE YEAR IS FITTINGLY CLOSED by the manifestation of Jesus in the synagogue of Nazareth as the fulfilment of prophecy. The words of grace which He spoke, after declaring Himself to be this fulfilment, are not recorded ; but it will be observed that when He visited Nazareth at the close of the second year, what astonished the Nazarenes was His wisdom. His manifestation and words of grace are the foundation upon which wisdom builds. The work which Jesus Christ fulfilled in laying this foundation could not be relaid, or done away, or even altered (1 Cor. iii. 11, cp. Iren. i. 10, 2 ; iii. 12, 6). The Church was built upon this foundation stone, and this was the fulfilment of prophecy, as Jesus Himself said to the Pharisees : 'Have you never read in the Scriptures, the stone which the builders rejected, the same was made the head of the corner?' (Matt. xxi. 16). If this does not refer to Jesus Christ, we may well ask with Him, 'What then does this Scripture mean?' (Luke xx. 17).

Synoptical Table of the First Year.

1. *The Old Elements Vivified.*

	Matt.	Mark	Luke	John
On January 6, Jesus was baptised, when the Spirit descended on Him, and a Voice proclaimed Him God's Son.[1]	iii. 13-17	i. 9-11	iii. 21, 22	
He is next presented as enduring temptation forty days in the desert.	iv. 1-11	i. 12, 13	iv. 1-13	
On his return to John's company, John pointed Him out as the Lamb of God.				i. 29-51
At a marriage at Cana, Jesus manifested His glory by turning water (the Word in the old vessels) into wine.				ii. 1-12
At the Passover Jesus cleansed the Temple and, as a warrant, indicated its being raised up in His resurrection.				ii. 13-25

2. *The Birth by Water and the Spirit.*

				John
After the Passover or about Pentecost Jesus declared to Nicodemus the need				iii. 1-21

---

[1] The first word of the voice at Christ's baptism is differently given. St. Matthew's form begins, 'This is my Beloved Son' (iii. 17) ; but in St. Mark (i. 11) and St. Luke we read, 'Thou art my Beloved Son.' Now the Aramaic or Hebrew original admits of a form combining both these, beginning *Attah hu*, literally, 'Thou this' or 'Thou art he,' so that the voice was, 'Thou art he (this), my Beloved Son, in whom I am well pleased.' The idiom occurs in Isaiah xli. 4, where Jehovah says, *Ani hu*, 'I this,' or 'I am he.'

Matt. Mark Luke John

of a new birth, to see the kingdom of God.

3. *Jesus Baptises the People mediately.*

About the Feast of Tabernacles Jesus was baptising in Judea through His disciples and all men came to Him.[1]

iii.
22–36

4. *Messianic Prophecy Fulfilled.*

In December He declared Himself in Samaria to be Messiah, the Dispenser of living Water, and showed the harvest.

iv.
1–42

Soon after He healed the nobleman's son of Capernaum with a word of power,[2] and showed Himself in the Synagogue of Nazareth as the fulfilment of prophecy, but, being rejected by His countrymen, He went to settle at Capernaum.

iv.

	Matt.	Mark	Luke	John
Soon after...				iv. 43–54
and showed...	iv. 12	i. 14	iv. 14–30	
men, He went...	iv. 13–17		iv. 31	

THE SECOND YEAR OF CHRIST'S MINISTRY.

A.D. 28.

The Kingdom, its Laws, Apostles, Miracles of Healing, and Wisdom.

THE SETTLEMENT AT CAPERNAUM must have been about the beginning of Christ's second year's ministry. In December He came to Galilee, and His visits to Cana and some of the Synagogues of Galilee, including Nazareth, would, in all probability, occupy the rest of this year. With His settlement in a then populous centre He began a new era of His ministry by preaching, and He preached repentance, or a new mind, as the word (μετά-voια) etymologically means, and the Gospel of the Kingdom of God, which, as He afterwards said, is within men. Formerly, He had had disciples; He now called men to be trained as missionary agents. The year is characterised as a year of plain, preceptive, and illustrative teaching. It was thus the Pentecostal year of Christ's ministry, and Pentecost was the feast He attended.

[1] Two reasons are indicated why Jesus left Judea; one was the imprisonment of John (Matt. iv. 12), and the other was the jealousy of the Pharisees (John iv. 1–3). The one was not inconsistent with the other.

[2] It was perhaps to this miracle that the Nazarenes referred when they challenged Jesus to do at Nazareth what they had heard of His doing at Capernaum.

The Controversy about the Sabbath began, in all proba-' bility, about the time of the Passover of the second year, for the Passover was at the first beginning of harvest, at the time of the year when there would be ears of corn for the disciples to pluck and eat. Luke (vi. 1) tells us that they did so ' on the Sabbath the second-first ' (ἐν Σαββάτῳ δευτεροπρώτῳ), which might mean on the second-first Sabbath according to some reckoning of Sabbaths, or on a Sabbath, being the second-first day, according to some reckoning of days. The expression is applicable to the *second* day of the Passover, which was the first day of counting (*sephirah*), that is, in reckoning Pentecost, which was the fiftieth day or seven complete weeks after this day of counting. The second day of the Passover was, therefore, the second-the-first day of counting to Pentecost, and if it happened this year to be a Sabbath, it was 'Sabbath second-first' on which the ears of corn were plucked. Again, in counting the seven weeks after the second day of the Passover to Pentecost, the Jews probably counted the Sabbaths exactly as the Catholic Churches count the Sundays after Easter. There is some ground, therefore, for explaining '.Sabbath second-first ' as being the first Sabbath after the second day of the Passover. This explanation only puts the plucking of the ears of corn a few days later.

In defending the action of His disciples on the Sabbath, Jesus first referred to David's eating the shewbread and also giving it to his followers,[1] and then called Himself also ' Lord of the Sabbath.'

[1] Ahimelech was the high priest in whose days or in whose presence (as the Greek preposition ἐπί might be translated) David ate the shewbread. According to St. Mark (ii. 26), however, David ate the shewbread in the days of Abiathar the high priest, or, as the Revised Version reads, (a) chief priest. In 2 Sam. xx. 25, and most other passages of the Old Testament, Abiathar is described as the son of Ahimelech, and as high priest with Zadok after David came to be king ; but in 2 Sam. viii. 17, 1 Chron. xviii. 16, and 1 Chron. xxiv. 3, 6, 31, the names are transposed, Abiathar being represented as the father and Ahimelech as the son. It is shown by the pedigree of Josephus that many of his priestly ancestors bore the name of Matthias in succession (*Life*, 1, 2). Annas or Ananus had a son also called Annas, and also high priest (Jos. *Ant.* xx. 9, 1). It was also not uncommon for persons mentioned in the Old Testament to have two names, especially if they were priests. Five instances occur in 1 Macc. ii. 1-5. In this way the father of that Zacharias who was killed between the altar and the sanctuary (2 Chron. xxiv. 20 ; Matt. xxiii. 35) may have borne both the names Berechiah ('whom God blessed') and Jehoiada ('whom God knew'). The title translated high priest is also ambiguous, meaning both the high priest and a chief priest. Thus, though Joseph Caiaphas was the high priest in the time of Christ, yet his father-in-law, Annas, was a chief priest, and, in fact, the chief or leading priest (Luke iii. 2 ; Acts iv. 6 ; cp. *Wars*, Jos. iv. 3 ; 7). It seems unnecessary to suppose that he acted as *zagan* or substitute for the high priest, though he may have done so.

This does not merely mean that He had power to alter it ; there is also a reference to the significance of the Sabbath—namely, to that rest (literally Sabbatism) of God, which remained in David's time to the people of God, and upon which, according to the writer to the Hebrews, they who had believed on Christ were entering (Heb. iv. 1-11).. The Sabbath foreshadowed good things to come, but the body foreshadowed was Christ (Col. ii. 16, 17) ; and, in the very same sense, Jesus a little later in this year said, 'Come unto Me all ye who *labour* and are heavy laden and I will give you *rest.* Take My yoke upon you and learn of Me ; for I am meek and lowly in heart ; and ye shall find rest unto your souls' (Matt. xi. 28-30). The word here used for *rest* is a Greek word (ἀνάπαυσις), which in the Septuagint replaces *Shabbath* (pl.) (Lev. xxv. 5), and *Shabbaton* (Ex. xvi. 23, &c.) ; and the allusion to the Sabbath thus appears in the invitation of those who labour and are heavy laden. The nature of the rest or Sabbatism of God appears first in the institution of the Sabbath. The word *Shabath* means properly to 'sit down' (Gesenius) and then to 'rest ;' and when God is said to have finished His work, the Hebrew word (*killah*), translated 'finish,' has the double sense of our English word, meaning both to 'leave off' and also to 'complete' (cp. Gen. ii. 1 and Gen. vi. 16). God finished or completed His work on the seventh day by descending (sitting down) upon it and resting upon it or communicating Himself to His rational creatures, as the Spirit of God also 'brooded over' the waters at the beginning. Another proof that this is the meaning of the Sabbatism or rest of God is derived from the fulfilment of the Feast of Pentecost, when the Holy Spirit came and 'sat upon' each of the Apostles (Acts ii. 1, 2). This feast was also called the Feast of Weeks, or, as the Hebrew has it, the Feast of Sabbaths ; and, as we shall see, this was the feast which Jesus this year attended, and which characterises the year. According to St. Peter, 'the Spirit of God resteth upon those who in the name of Christ endure reproach and trials' (1 Pet. iv. 14), and this Spirit resting upon them is called by St. Paul 'the power of Christ resting upon them' (2 Cor. xii. 9). Now as it is by coming to Jesus Christ, by taking on His yoke and learning of Him, that the rest promised by Jesus is attained, it was proper that this declaration of Himself as the Lord of this Sabbatismal rest should be made at the Passover (the foundation feast) and in the year characterised by plain directions and lessons, the year when, as we shall now see, He attended the Feast of Sabbaths (Weeks).

THE UNNAMED FEAST, mentioned in John v., was probably Pentecost. All would admit that the miracle done at it, and the discourse following the miracle, relate to the Sabbath question, and that this connection gives some ground for presuming that it was either Pentecost or the Passover. The alternative reading, 'the feast of the Jews,' instead of 'a feast of the Jews,' would favour the idea that it was the Passover, or the Feast of Tabernacles, which was often called 'the Feast' (Edersheim, ii. 149). But the following reasons make it probable that it was Pentecost.[1] First, if the second-first day, or second day of the Passover, and first of counting to Pentecost, was a Sabbath, then the following day of Pentecost was also a Sabbath ; and this agrees with the fact that the unnamed feast was a Sabbath. Secondly, there is a great probability that the feast in question was one of the three great feasts of the Jews. Every Jew in Palestine was expected to be at one at least of these feasts every year ; and, if he lived near Jerusalem, he was expected to be at all three. But if this feast was not one of these three, then there would be no record of the presence of Jesus at any one of them during this second year, which, as we have seen, cannot be omitted. But if John had meant that Jesus was present at the Passover, or the Feast of Tabernacles, he would probably have named the feast, whereas Pentecost had scarcely any proper name of its own, being called the Fiftieth day (*Pentecostê*) after the Passover. It was, indeed, called the Feast of Weeks, or Sabbaths ; but either this expressed its being seven weeks after the Passover, or it indicated some special connection with God's rest, in which case there would be a propriety in healing the impotent man at it. Thirdly, John apparently represents Jesus as present during His first year's ministry at the Passover, during His second at Pentecost, and during His third at the Feast of Tabernacles (McClellan's 'Four Gospels,' pp. 460, 546, n. 6). Fourthly, when Jesus delivered the Sermon on the Mount, He was followed by such crowds from Idumea, Perea, Phœnicia, &c., as would be present at Jerusalem during the beautiful season of Pentecost. Fifthly, the expression, 'the hour is coming and now is' (John v. 25), seems to indicate the season when the Holy Spirit came—that is, Pentecost (Acts ii. 1, 2). The feast was limited to one day ; and its distinguishing rite was the offering of the two first loaves of wheaten bread, *made*

---

[1] Chrysostom, Cyril, Tatian, Calvin, Bengel, Lewin, Friedlieb, Townsend, McClellan, Skene, and Vaihinger in Herzog's Encyclopædia, think that this unnamed feast was Pentecost ; Irenæus and many others have thought it was the Passover, which concluded in Pentecost (Jos. *Ant.* iii. 10, 6). Others, including those who would not count this year, represent the unknown feast as the Feast of Purim in March, or some feast towards the close of the preceding year.

with leaven (Lev. xxiii. 17), and, along with two lambs of the first year, waved before the Lord.

THE SERMON ON THE MOUNT was in all probability delivered immediately after the Feast of Pentecost ; it corresponds to the Sinaitic Law, or the Ten Commandments, which, according to the Jewish tradition, were also given at this season. St. Matthew places this Sermon before certain miracles and events which really preceded it. In his plan of grouping it has been suggested that he followed the order of the Old Testament history, first giving the Genesis part of the Gospel ; then the Exodus of the Child Jesus from Egypt ; then the account of Christ's forty days' fast after the manner of Moses ; and then, immediately after this, the plain precepts of Christianity, promulgated at the Mountain, as the plain precepts of Judaism were promulgated at Mount Sinai. Even according to St. Matthew (vii. 28, R.V.), parts of the Sermon on the Mount were delivered in the hearing of 'the multitudes' (ὄχλοι, wrongly translated 'people' in A.V.), that is, 'on the level place' where they were, below the summit of the mountain. These parts, as recorded by St. Luke, apply to all men. To the introductory Beatitudes St. Luke's account adds woes. Then we have in it the law of charity or kindness to all men, the golden rule, the danger of blind guidance, the necessity for a tolerant, forgiving, and good spirit, and the folly of calling Jesus Lord without doing what He says. The other parts may have been spoken more apart, as they seem more applicable to teachers ; and St. Luke, though he does not give them in the Sermon, recapitulates most of them in his peculiar section towards the close of Christ's ministry. In these the disciples are called the salt of the earth and the light of the world, and exhorted to let their good works appear. It was not to set aside the divine commandments that Jesus professed to come, but to enable men to keep them more perfectly in thought and word as well as in outward conduct, and therefore He required that the righteousness of the disciples should exceed the righteousness of the Scribes and Pharisees. The Sinaitic commandments, 'Thou shalt not kill, &c.' must be fulfilled in the thoughts and intents of the heart. In their alms, and prayers, and fastings, they were to avoid hypocritical pretences, and as a specimen of prayer we have the Lord's Prayer. They were not to have their principal interest in the things of this life, so as to hide or misrepresent the truth (the light), because of Mammon worship, or because of undue anxieties about such things as food or clothing, but to enter in by the narrow gate of the straitened way that leadeth to life. Finally, though he who both does God's commandments and teaches others shall be called great in the kingdom of heaven, yet to many who prophesy in Christ's name and who yet work, iniquity, He will profess that He never *knew* them. We can well believe, therefore, that these latter parts, bearing on the duties and dangers of religious teachers, would be spoken by Christ apart on the Mountain, and recapitulated towards the close of His ministry.

THE FIRST SERIES OF PARABLES, called the 'Boat Parables,' begins with the Parable of the Sower. This is considered to indicate that the seed was then being sown or about to be sown, and this would be about the time of the Feast of Tabernacles, in the beginning of October or shortly after. The preceptive teaching which characterises the year is appropriately completed by these parables, because they embody the plain directions of such discourses as the Sermon on the Mount in figures borrowed from ordinary life, and requiring an exercise of thought. Milk, or elementary teaching, is for children ; men of riper growth need stronger food, which requires more elaborate digestion. Mysteries also serve as a discipline for the multitudes, to still that sea ; and, in speaking the Parables, Jesus 'sat upon the sea.' The seven or eight parables, given all together by St. Matthew in chap. xiii., were probably not all spoken on the same day. St. Luke gives only the Parable of the Sower in this connection, and places those of the Mustard Seed and the Leaven in his recapitulatory section (xiii. 18-21). The explanation of the first parable was given privately to Christ's disciples (Mark iv. 33, R.V.), and, in addition, He spoke to them three parables concerning the Hid Treasure, the Pearl of Great Price, and the Sweep-net. These three parables are given only by St. Matthew (xiii. 44-52), and from his words (v. 53) and Mark vi. 1 we infer that, some time after completing the series, Jesus visited Nazareth a second time.[1]

THE LESSON WHICH JESUS APPENDS to the last of these parables, that of the Sweep-net, indicates the perfection of that teaching which characterises this year. 'Every (learned) Scribe,' He said, 'who has been trained for or indoctrinated ($\mu\alpha\theta\eta\tau\epsilon\upsilon\theta\epsilon\iota\varsigma$) in the kingdom of heaven is like a Man, the Master of a House, who brings forth from His treasures things new and old' (Matt. xiii. 52). It is for such a learned teacher to work up the parabolic and mysterious, together with and by means of what is plain and incontrovertible, so as to present the old faith in the new form of a full-grown science ; he builds upon the old basis a superstructural system, but he does not destroy or undermine the old basis on which he is building. Fittingly, Jesus Christ presents

---

[1] So Wieseler, Tischendorf, Meyer, Stier, Robinson, Townsend, Ellicott, Godet, Andrews, Keil, Edersheim, Greswell, Patritius, Lewin, Thomson, Ewald.

Himself at the close of this second year again in the Synagogue of Nazareth, speaking words of marvellous wisdom and having marvellous powers. These form the consummation of the second year which begins with the preaching of a kingdom coming within men's minds, which next sets forth Jesus Christ as Lord and Giver of Sabbatic rest, then gives directive precepts to be followed and lessons to be learned in order to enter into this rest, then parables suitable to a riper age, and lastly shows the wisdom and powers of the Master of the House, who Himself said that nothing is hidden (in parabolic mysteries) but that it might be made manifest (Mark iv. 22, R.V.).

Synoptical Table of the Second Year.

1. *The new mind of God's Kingdom.*

	Matt.	Mark	Luke	John
About the beginning of January Jesus began at Capernaum to preach repentance (change of mind), and called the four fishermen (Simon, Andrew, James and John) to be fishers of men.	iv. 13–17 iv. 18–22	i. 14, 15 16–20		
In the Synagogue He rebuked, silenced, and cast out an unclean spirit.[1]		i. 21–28	iv. 31–37	
He then healed Peter's wife's mother of a great fever, and others diseased.	viii. 14–17	i. 29–34	iv. 38–41	
In beginning a circuit in Galilee, He gave a miraculous draught of fishes.	iv. 23–25	i. 35–39	iv. 42 –v. 11	
A leper, being healed, so noised the matter about, that Jesus had to withdraw.	viii. 2–4	i. 40–45	v. 12–16	
Returning to Capernaum, after some months' circuit, He healed the paralytic.	ix. 1–8	ii. 1–12	v. 17–26	
Matthew, the publican, was now called; but the feast in his house was later.[2]	ix. 9–17	ii. 13–22	v. 27–39	

[1] Our English versions of the New Testament speak of men 'being possessed with devils' or 'possessed with a devil;' but the original Greek word is demonised (δαιμονιζόμενοι). St. James speaks of a wisdom that is demoniacal or demon-like (δαιμονιώδης). The New Testament writers also speak of men being 'in an unclean spirit' (Mark i. 23), or having devils or demons (Luke viii. 27); of demons being cast out or coming out of men, and St. Luke speaks of Satan entering into Judas Iscariot (Luke xxii. 3). We still speak of men being bedevilled, or bewitched, or possessed, or not being themselves. It is hard to say what is the efficient cause of such an abnormal state; and, as Irenæus says (ii. 28, 7), 'the cause itself of the nature of transgressors neither hath any Scripture related, nor apostle said, nor hath the Lord taught; and consequently we must leave this knowledge to God, lest we frame an impious antitheistic hypothesis.'

[2] In Hebrew and Hellenistic narration, *and* does not always imply

2. *The Sabbath rest and the Sermon.*   Matt.   Mark Luke John

	Matt.	Mark	Luke	John
On the second day of THE PASSOVER,	xii.	ii.	vi.	
a Sabbath, or on the first Sabbath after	1-8	23-28	1-5	
it, the disciples plucked ears of corn.				
This, and the healing of the man with	xii.	iii.	vi.	
the withered hand on another Sabbath,	9-14	1-6	6-11	
and of the impotent man at Bethesda, at				v.
Pentecost, provoked the Pharisees.				1-47
AFTER PENTECOST, multitudes followed	xii.	iii.		
Jesus to a Mount near the sea of Galilee.	15-21	7-12		
Here He appointed the Twelve	v. 1	iii.	vi.	
Apostles, and delivered the great Sermon.	-vii.	13-19	12-49	
He then healed the servant of the	viii.		vii.	
centurion, who approached Him by means	5-13		1-10	
of the elders of the Jews.[1]				

immediate or even chronological sequence. The feast which Matthew made for Jesus appears not to have been at the time of his call, but when Jairus came the second time to tell Jesus that his daughter was dead. St. Matthew's connectives indicate that it was *then* (ix. 14), upon this feast that Jesus discoursed on the impropriety of patching an old garment with new cloth, and that 'while he spake these things unto them' Jairus came. But Jairus had come shortly before, when Jesus was by the seaside, to say that his daughter was dying (Mark v. 21, 23 ; Luke viii. 40, 42); and, as in the case of Lazarus, Jesus seems to have waited till the girl was dead. Jairus then came a second time to Jesus as He discoursed in Matthew's house. St. Luke also (v. 27-39) gives the discourse about patching an old garment and in connection with this feast. It may be here observed that St. Luke's word (σχίζει or σχίσει) translated in the Authorised Version 'maketh a rent,' is in the Revised Version translated 'he will rend (the new '), so as to introduce another reason. But, even if we accept the Revised translation, one reason does not exclude the other. Both reasons may well have been assigned.

[1] In the Greek of Matthew's account (viii. 5) the compound verb (προσέρχομαι) with the dative is translated 'come to,' but in the Septuagint, or ancient Greek translation of the Old Testament, which is the basis of much of the New Testament diction, this compound (προσέρχομαι) not unseldom replaces two Hebrew verbs, nagash and karabh, both meaning 'to draw near' or 'approach.' It replaces nagash in Gen. xxix. 10 ; xliii. 19 ; Lev. xxi. 21 ; Deut. xxi. 5 ; and karabh in Num. ix. 6 ; Deut. i. 22 ; Lev. xxi. 16. Instead of this Greek word, we have sometimes the Greek ἐγγίζειν (Cremer). Now as Matthew wrote his Gospel originally in Hebrew, the question comes to be, what Hebrew verb in his original was translated by this Greek compound (προσέρχομαι). In the two modern Hebrew versions of the New Testament, Delitzsch's and Salkinson-Ginsburg's, nagash is put for it in Matt. viii. 5. In all probability, therefore, nagash or karabh was the verb which the Greek translator of Matthew's Hebrew or Aramaic had before him. He was no doubt well acquainted with the Septuagint language, but even in ordinary language the Greek compound had the sense opposite to ἀπέρχομαι, to go away. If, therefore, Matthew's original word was nagash, all that he says is that the centurion 'approached' Jesus. He does not, like

	Matt.	Mark	Luke	John
And raised the widow's son at Nain— the first resurrection miracle of Jesus.			vii. 11–17	
John the Baptist, hearing of these things, sent to inquire if Jesus were the Messiah, and was shown healing miracles.	xi. 2, 3		vii. 18–20	
Jesus then compared unsophisticated learners to babes, promising rest to such.	xi. 4–30		vii. 21–35	
A woman, whose sins had been pardoned, anointed Jesus' feet, as He sat at meat in Simon the Pharisee's house.			vii. 36–50	
Connected with these events was the second circuit in Galilee.			viii. 1–3	

3. *The Parabolic Teaching of Christ.*

	Matt.	Mark	Luke	John
The Pharisees denounced the healing of a demonised deaf and dumb man and other miracles of Jesus as due to a league with Beelzebub.	xii. 22–37	iii. 20–30	cp. xi. 14–26	
His friends and relatives also beginning to doubt His sanity, came more than once seeking Him in the crowd.	xii. 46–50	iii. 21, 31–35	viii. 19–21	
About the Feast of Tabernacles, or seed-time, Jesus spoke the Boat Parables:	xiii. 1, 2	iv. 1, 2	viii. 4	
The Sower, the Wheat and the Darnels (Tares), the Mustard Seed and the Leaven; afterwards, apart to His disciples, those of the Hid Treasure, the Pearl and the Net, with explanations.	xiii. 3–35 xiii. 36–50	iv. 3–34	viii. 5–18 cp. xiii. 18–21	
Crossing the Sea of Galilee, He stilled the storm ; and, on landing at Gerasa,	viii. 23–27	iv. 35–41	viii. 22–35	

St. Luke, tell us how. The direct form of address, given by St. Matthew, does not prove that the centurion was in the presence of Jesus ; for St. Luke gives the centurion's message also in the first person : 'Neither thought I myself worthy to come unto Thee' (Luke vii. 7). Here Matthew's compound is not used, but the simple uncompounded words (πρός σε ἐλθεῖν), which mean to come literally to one, to come into one's presence, and are replaced in the two Hebrew versions by the common Hebrew verb to go or come (bō' eleycha, or bō' l'pancycha). When again, at the close, St. Matthew represents Jesus as saying to the centurion, 'Go thy way,' it is to be observed first, that the expression is valedictory, and means something like 'Go on thy way,' for when Blind Bartimæus was so addressed, he followed Jesus in the way (Mark x. 52). Secondly, it is not certain from St. Luke's account that Jesus did not after all call at the centurion's house, which 'he was not far from ' (Luke vii. 6), or that the messages did not end in an interview,

	Matt.	Mark	Luke	John
He healed two demoniacs, allowing[1] the	viii.	v.	viii.	
demons to go into a herd of swine.	28-34	1-20	26-39	
Returning to Capernaum, He was en-	ix.	v.	viii,	
tertained by Matthew, healed the woman	18-26	21-43	40-56	
having an issue of blood, raised Jairus'	ix.	vi.		
daughter, healed two blind men and a	27-38	6		
dumb demoniac.				

4. The wisdom of the Master-Scribe.

	Matt.	Mark	Luke	John
In completing this series of parables,	xiii.			
Jesus compared the well-qualified teacher	51, 52			
to a Man, the Master of a House, bring-				
ing forth things new and old.				
Coming to Nazareth, during a third	xiii.	vi.		
circuit, He taught in the Synagogue with	53-58	1-6		
astonishing wisdom and power.				

THE THIRD YEAR'S MINISTRY.

A.D. 29.

Veiled Mediated teaching: provision for the multitudes in the desert.

This was the year in which Jesus attended the Feast of Tabernacles, and this feast was the commemoration of the Israelites' life in the wilderness or desert. Before they entered upon their inheritance or land of promise, they passed through a training of enduring hardships. First, it was in the desert that Jesus at the Passover and at Pentecost fed the thousands, so that the analogy of the food He gave them to the manna of the desert presented itself to the Jews. On other occasions throughout the year, as when He withdrew from those who would have made Him king, and from those who asked a sign from heaven, when again He sought concealment in Syro-Phœnicia (Mark vii. 24), when He healed the blind man of Bethsaida privately, in the silence of the Gospels about His presence and doings both before and after the Feast of Tabernacles, in His withdrawal during it, in His retiring after the Feast of Dedication back again to the place where John first baptised (John x. 40), the same course of retiring from open manifestation, and of leading His followers into the wilderness, appears prominently. Secondly, the idea of a delegated ministry in dealing with the multitudes characterises the period. In dealing

---

[1] The Greek word (ἐπιτρέπω) means no more than that Jesus suffered the demons to go, did not hinder them. One demoniac was the chief actor.

with untrained and gross-minded men, Jesus Himself warned His agents not to cast pearls before swine ; and St. Paul charges Titus (ii. 15) to let no man despise him. In explaining to such men the transparently clear truths hidden in mysteries, it is possible to provoke their ridicule, and perhaps cause them to lose the superficial knowledge they have, although to minds above their level or better prepared 'no subject could be more admirable or inspiring' (Clem. Alex. 'S.' i. 12, v. 8–10). To prepare the people the Apostles were like the Seventy 'sent to be before His face to every city and place where He Himself was about to come' (Luke x. 1) ; for when He had ended His charge to them He departed to teach and to preach in *their* cities (Matt. xi. 1). Their mission was thus to prepare the way for that fuller en-lightenment which was proper to their Master's direct teaching. The third year must have commenced with their mission, for they returned shortly before the Passover in April (Nisan), when Jesus withdrew with them to the desert place belonging to Bethsaida Julias, and there fed the Five Thousand (cp. Mark vi. 30, 31 with John vi. 4). The terms of their commission, their statements on their return, and Christ's corresponding circuit (Matt xi. 1), indicate that they must have been absent several weeks (Andrews), about two months (Archbishop Thomson), less (Greswell), or more. It follows that they were sent out about the commencement of the third year's ministry in January. The connection of the history is, therefore, as follows. After a circuit of teaching in all the cities and villages (Matt. ix. 35 ; Mark vi. 7), including Nazareth, Jesus seeing how 'the multitudes were worried (distressed) and tossed (to and fro or aside), as sheep not having a shepherd, was moved with compassion for them.' 'The harvest is truly plentiful,' He said to the disciples, bidding them pray that the Lord of the harvest would send forth labourers into His harvest (Matt. ix. 36–38). The Mission of the Apostles followed. When, after their return, He withdrew into the desert or wilderness, He, like Moses, led the multitudes after Him into the desert, and there fed them with suitable food. The idea of a delegated or mediated ministry again appears in the employment of the disciples to convey the food to the multitudes in both miracles ; and the same idea is also indicated at the Feast of Tabernacles, when, in allusion to the water-pouring, Jesus invited the thirsty to come to Him and drink, and declared that the recipient would become a means of conveying the water to others (John vii. 38). Thirdly, Jesus this year extended His own sphere of work, visiting Syro-Phœnicia, probably the Lebanon district, Bashan, and Perea ; the year's ministry was more cosmopolitan.

Fourthly, the Feast of Tabernacles, which Jesus this year attended, besides celebrating the desert life of Israel, was characterised by extraordinary sacrifices of bullocks. It was a feast of strong meat, fit for men's digestion. So also the loaves and fishes, on which the multitudes were fed, were solid meat, not elementary milk (cp. 1 Cor. iii. 2 ; Heb. v. 14) ; and Jesus bade His disciples take heed what leaven they mingled with this bread. Unless He had given them to understand that He meant doctrine, critics might have said that leaven means only leaven, and that doctrine means doctrine, but we must allow Jesus to explain Himself. The same characteristics run through all Christ's utterances during this year. Instead of such teaching as the Sermon on the Mount, we have only deep or enigmatic utterances, requiring full-grown digestion. As men's minds advance to maturity, there is a training by means of 'the deep things of God,' if men study them soberly ; and there is no royal (or easy) road to learning them.

AFTER THE FEEDING OF THE FIVE THOUSAND, Jesus discoursed at Capernaum on the Bread of Life and on eating with unwashen hands. He then withdrew to the borders of Syro-Phœnicia, and, according to the Revised Version, returned by Sidon, which included the Lebanon district.

THE FEEDING OF THE FOUR THOUSAND took place probably about the time of Pentecost in 'the Mountain,' and in Grecianised Decapolis. At Pentecost there would be crowds passing through that district to and from Jerusalem ; and if we suppose that the miracle occurred at any other season, farther on in summer, it would be difficult to account for their presence. The mention made by Jesus of leaven in connection with the Bread, also indicates that the miracle took place about Pentecost, for it was specially directed that the two wheaten loaves of the Pentecostal offering were to be baked with leaven (Lev. xxiii. 17). Jesus Himself gave His disciples to understand that by leaven He meant doctrine or teaching, admonishing them to beware of the old leaven of the Pharisees and Sadducees (Matt. xvi. 11, 12). Pentecost, we know, was fulfilled in the coming of the Holy Spirit—the Spirit of a sound, well-regulated, and sober mind ;[1]

---

[1] Compare Rom. xii. 3, on the Greek μὴ ὑπερφρονεῖν παρ' ὃ δεῖ φρονεῖν, ἀλλὰ φρονεῖν εἰς τὸ σωφρονεῖν, 'not to think transcendentally beyond the proper sphere of man's thinking, but to think so as to be soberly thoughtful.' St. Paul cautioned his converts against the wild speculations of his age (1 Cor. iii. 20), which afterwards in the shape of the Gnostic heresies troubled the Church. They were founded on mere fancies about God's physical infinity, the cause of evil, the distribution of natures physically to men, &c. We must still beware of such transcendental leaven, as well as of the leaven of the Pharisees and the Sadducees.

C

and this wisdom from above is needed to interpret rightly the
hidden mystery of Christ (1 Cor. ii. 7). No other foundation
can be laid but Jesus Christ; but men must take heed not to
build perishable materials or such rubbish as stubble upon this
foundation (1 Cor. iii. 10-13), not to misconstrue 'the enigma'
(1 Cor. xiii. 12). The offering at the Passover was mere flour,
but the offering at Pentecost was flour baked, so to speak, into a
solid system, by means of leaven, which represents doctrine,
characterised by 'imperishableness, gravity, sound irreprehensible
discourse' (Tit. ii. 8), and sobermindedness.

AFTER SENDING THE MULTITUDES AWAY, Jesus crossed by
boat to the western side. Here the Pharisees and the Sadducees,
now acting in conjunction, asked of Him a sign from heaven.
He referred to the history of Jonah the prophet, and immediately
recrossed to the eastern side of the Galilean Lake, moving northward till He came to Bethsaida Julias, where He healed a blind
man privately. In this neighbourhood, that is, in Bashan and
Galilee (cp. John vii. 9), He probably moved about till the
Feast of Tabernacles on the 15th of Tisri, in the beginning of
October.

AT THE FEAST OF TABERNACLES (Tisri 15-22=October 12-19)
Jesus went up to Jerusalem (John vii. 2-10). This feast corresponded with the conclusion of the whole harvest, when the figs
were gathered and the vintage ended. It celebrated the tent life
which the Israelites had led in the wilderness, the people now
dwelling in booths (tabernacles) made on the roofs of their
houses out of the branches of olive, palm, myrtle, and other fat
('*aboth*) trees, while they carried in one hand a palm or *lûlabh*,
made of a palm, a myrtle, and a willow branch tied together, and,
in their other hand, an *æthrog* or paradise apple — a sort of
citron, as the fruit of goodly trees (Lev. xxiii. 40, R.V.). A leafy
canopy of willows was also made round the altar. On each of the
seven days water was brought from the pool of Siloam, and poured
out, along with the wine of the libation, into two silver basins at
the top of the altar slope. After this water-pouring, the Great
Hallel (Ps. cxiii.-cxviii.) was chanted, with responses and flute
music, closing with a procession round the altar. Thirteen
bullocks were sacrificed on the first day, twelve on the second,
and so on—seventy in all. At night the Temple was brilliantly
illuminated, and there was great rejoicing in it. On the seventh
day the procession was made seven times round the altar, and
then the booths were dismantled. On the eighth day there was
a holy convocation or assembly without any of the special
services of the previous week. Christ's attendance at this feast

was not with a view to manifest Himself openly (John vii. 4-18). He went up to it in secret. He did appear teaching in the Temple about the midst of the feast, but not on the first two days, which were the most sacred part. His doctrine, He said, was His Father's—not His own ; He spake not 'of (from) Himself,' nor was the Holy Spirit to speak 'of Himself' (John xvi. 13). Truth is truth. In reference to the water-pouring, He invited the thirsty to come to Him and drink, and declared that those who believed in Him would become sources whence living water would flow, and that those who kept His word would not taste of death for ever. In reference to the Temple illumination, He called Himself the Light of the world, and spoke of the darkness which the rejection of this light involved, as being itself a judgment. The judgment, He said, was not by His express interference, but according to truth (John viii. 16). When His words, ' Before Abraham was, I am,' brought Him into peril of being stoned (John viii. 58, 59), He concealed Himself, but in then disappearing (παράγων translated *passing by*), He gave sight to the man born blind, who confessed his healer to be the Son of God, while the self-conceited Pharisees shut their eyes to the plainest miraculous evidence, and were so made blind (John ix. 39). When Jesus afterwards spoke to them about His sheep, the Door, and the Good Shepherd, we have another indication of concealment, for John tells us (x. 6) that ' they knew not what the things were which He spake to them.' We conclude that Christ's visit to the Feast of Tabernacles was in keeping with the veiled presentation of the Divine Word, which characterises the third year's ministry, serving both to stimulate the minds of more advanced seekers after truth and to discipline the multitudes. This character was typified in the covering of booths, under which Israel, God's Son, lived for seven days at this Feast.

THE INTERVAL between the Feast of Tabernacles in October and the Feast of Dedication (Kisleu 25-Tebeth 2 = December 20-27) was in all probability spent by Jesus in retired seclusion.[1] Although some harmonists—as Lichtenstein and Andrews —imagine that the Transfiguration took place in this interval, and others—as Ellicott and Tischendorf—place the Mission of the Seventy in it ; yet there is good reason for believing that these events followed the Feast of Dedication, and introduced the fourth year's ministry. There is abundance of time for them after both the feasts. At all events, nothing is known for certain about the doings of Jesus during this interval. As Jesus, after the

---

[1] Greswell, Wieseler, Robinson, Stroud, Lewin, Kitto, and McClellan put nothing into this interval between the feasts.

Feast of Dedication, went back again (πάλιν) to the place where John first baptised, it might be inferred with some probability that He was there during the interval between the feasts. This place was in all probability some part of Bashan, the wilderness of Judea beyond Jordan. But wherever this interval of retirement from public life was spent, Jesus reappeared at the Feast of Dedication, openly declaring Himself to be the Son of God and one with the Father.

THE FEAST OF DEDICATION, at which Jesus reappeared, was instituted by Judas Maccabæus in B.C. 164, to purify and rededicate the Temple after its pollution by Antiochus Epiphanes (1 Macc. iv. 52-59). It was a joyous and even hilarious festivity, resembling the Feast of Tabernacles in lasting eight days, in the chanting of the Hallel, and originally (2 Macc. x. 7) but not latterly, in the practice of carrying palm branches. Not only the Temple, but every house in Jerusalem was brilliantly lighted up ; and hence the feast is called the Feast of Lights. Being then asked by the Jews to tell them plainly whether He were the Christ, He said that He had already told them, but that they had not believed, not being of His sheep ; that His sheep heard His voice and followed Him, and in so doing obtained eternal life. He added, ' I and my Father are one ' (thing). The Jews then took up stones to stone Him for blasphemy, but He justified His words by a quotation from Psalm lxxxii. 6, to the effect that the Scripture, which cannot be broken, gave the name of Gods to those to whom the Word of God came. He also appealed to His miracles. When the Jews still sought to arrest Him, He went forth out of their hand, and withdrew to the place where John first baptised. This we shall presently see was either on the way to Cæsarea Philippi, or perhaps it was a district of Bashan in which Cæsarea Philippi was, the 'parts' or 'villages' under Philip (Matt. xvi. 13 ; Mark viii. 27). On the way thither He asked His disciples, ' Who do men say that I, the Son of Man, am ? ' and then, ' Who do ye say that I am?' Peter replied, ' Thou art the Christ, the Son of the Living God.'[1] Jesus, in approving Peter's answer, declared that He would build His church upon this stone of confession connected, as we shall see, with Peter, and that the gates of Hades (death) would not prevail against it. The Son of God became Man that those ' who heard His voice and followed Him might have eternal life,' that they might partake of the divine nature of sonship, ' being purified and

---

[1] The full question and the full answer are given by St. Matthew, as in the Authorised Version. Jesus had often called Himself the Son of Man.

raised into the life of God' (Irenæus v. 9, 2), and that they might thus be one in God (John xvii. 11, 21, 22, 23). The psalm which Jesus quoted, speaks of God as 'standing in the congregation of God,' and as judging among the Gods. It calls Gods those who, attending with all diligence to God's Word, receive this baptism of the Word (Clem. Alex. 'Pæd.' i. 6), or ingrafting into Christ (Iren. v. 10), and participate in the Spirit dispensed through the Word, who keep this ingrafting by means of conduct conducive to the growth of the new nature. Men thus become blended with the Word, into which they are grafted, and with the Spirit given, (Iren. v. 6), so as to receive the divine sonship or become sons of God (iv. 38, 4). The 'congregation of God,' according to Irenæus, is the Church (Iren. iii. 6, 1). Christians form the Temple of God, and in them God dwells (1 Cor. iii. 16; vi. 19); but let them not, as individuals, defile the Temple of their own bodies, or, as a Church, apostatise from the love of truth, for then the psalm says that, though they have been called Gods, they 'shall yet die like men.' They must beware lest they follow the type of those Israelites in the wilderness with whom God was not well-pleased, and who, though redeemed from Egypt, were yet destroyed in the wilderness (1 Cor. x. 1–11).

Synoptical Table of the Third Year.

1. The Mission of the Apostles.	Matt.	Mark	Luke	John
About the beginning of January the apostles were sent out on their healing and teaching mission. ;[1] and Jesus Himself followed them.	x. 1–42 xi. 1	vi. 6–13	ix. 1–6	
Shortly before the Passover, the apostles returned ; and John's disciples came after Herod had murdered John while celebrating the day of his birth or accession.	xiv. 1–12	vi. 14–31	ix. 7–10	vi. 1–4

[1] It was no part of the commission of the apostles, says Dean Burgon, to 'raise the dead.' The Revisers left the clause because they found it in the corrupt, though ancient, manuscripts ℵ, B, C, D, and in the Latin versions. Not more manuscripts than one in twenty contain it. P. E. Pusey found it in no Syriac Version; and it is omitted by Eusebius, Basil, Chrysostom, Jerome, and Juvencus (*Revision Revised*, p. 108). The apostles were enjoined not to take 'staves' with them—that is, rods (ῥάβδους) for tenting purposes. Even if we accept the very questionable reading in Matt. x. 10, R.V., and Luke ix. 3, R.V., and read with the Revisers 'nor staff,' instead of 'nor staves,' as in the Authorised and Bishop Wordsworth's texts, we must still understand that Jesus forbade any rod or 'stick' for tenting purposes. It is unnatural to suppose that Jesus would forbid them to take the usual traveller's staff, which Mark expressly tells us (vi. 8) He permitted. There is the same ambiguity in our word 'stick.'

2. The Bread of Life in the Desert, and the Leaven of Doctrine.

	Matt.	Mark	Luke	John
ABOUT THE PASSOVER Jesus fed the five thousand in a desert near Bethsaida.	xiv. 13-21	vi. 32-44	ix. 11-17	vi. 5-15
After sending the disciples away, He followed the ship, walking on the sea.	xiv. 22-36	vi. 45-56		vi. 16-21
At Capernaum He discoursed to the returned crowds on the Bread of Life.				vi. 22-71
Answering a charge of eating with unwashed hands, He showed what defiles.	xv. 1-20	vii. 1-23		
After this He went to the Syro-Phœnician borders seeking concealment, and healed a Canaanitish woman's daughter.	xv. 21-28	vii. 24-30		
Returning probably by the Lebanon district, He healed a deaf-mute apart and others brought by the multitudes.	xv. 29-31			
ABOUT PENTECOST Jesus fed the four thousand in Grecianised Decapolis.	xv. 32-39	viii. 1-9		
Crossing in a boat to Dalmanutha, He gave the Pharisees the sign of Jonah.	xvi. 1-4	viii. 10-13		
Recrossing, He warned the disciples against the leaven of the Pharisees.	xvi. 5-12	viii. 14-21		
Coming to Bethsaida Julias, He restored sight to a blind man at two stages.		viii. 22-26		

3. At the Feast of Tabernacles.

	John
After some months spent in this Bashan district and in Galilee, Jesus went up to THE FEAST OF TABERNACLES secretly, not courting notoriety.	vii. 1 vii. 2-13
He then discoursed in the Temple, promising living water and indicating the judgment attending a life after the flesh and the rejection of light. Attempts to arrest and stone Him failed.	vii. 14-53 viii.
In withdrawing into concealment, He gave sight to the man born blind ; and, contrasting Himself with the hirelings, called Himself the Good Shepherd.	ix. x. 1-21

4. At the Feast of Dedication.

	John
An interval of seclusion followed, during which He was probably beyond Jordan, but nothing is known about Him.	x. 22

	Matt.	Mark	Luke	John

At the close of the year, Jesus reappeared in the Temple at the Feast of Dedication, and being asked if He were the Christ, called Himself the Son of God, one with the Father. — John x. 23–38

Being in danger of arrest He withdrew to the place where John first baptised. — John x. 39–42.

THE FOURTH YEAR'S MINISTRY.
A.D. 30.

The fulfilment of the days of Ascension.

THE FOURTH YEAR OF CHRIST'S MINISTRY may be reckoned from His departure from the Feast of Dedication, which lasted eight days, and ended this year on December 27, or on the 2nd of Thebet (the Jewish January). This marks the beginning of the fourth year independently of the date assigned to the Transfiguration, but the available evidence leads us to place the Transfiguration immediately after the Feast of Dedication, and to represent it as the fitting precursor to Christ's sufferings and the glory into which He entered through them. It is admitted, for instance, by Andrews, that, so far as the accounts in St. Matthew and St. Mark go, the Transfiguration may have occurred at any time between the miracle at Bethsaida Julias, subsequent to the feeding of the Four Thousand, and the next March or the payment of the Temple Tribute, claimed from every Israelite a month before the Passover. It is quite needless to bring in the supposition that these Temple dues were the arrears of the previous year, and paid by Jesus in September, before He went to the Feast of Tabernacles (Greswell). The reason for thus putting back the payment by Jesus of these Temple dues seems to be the mistaken idea that St. Luke places the Mission of the Seventy after the payment of them. St. Luke certainly places this Mission, as we shall see, after the reasoning about pre-eminence, but not necessarily after Christ's rebuke at Capernaum, some time subsequent to the reasoning. There is abundance of time for the Mission of the Seventy after the reasoning about pre-eminence, if we date the Transfiguration about the beginning of the year, and the reasoning, by the way, shortly after it. The first reason [1] for so dating the Transfiguration is that the conversation of Jesus

---

[1] MacClellan's reasons are here given. Bengel and Stier (in preface to Mark and Luke) place the Transfiguration and the Mission of the Seventy after the departure of Jesus from the Feast of Dedication. The arrangement here is similar. See also Baumgarten's *Geschichte Jesu.*

with Moses and Elias referred to the Exodus (imperfectly translated 'decease' or 'departure') which Jesus was to 'fulfil' at
Jerusalem (Luke ix. 31) ; and, as this certainly referred to the
Passover, there is reason to believe that the next great feast
after the conversation was the Passover, and not the Feast of
Tabernacles, or even that of Dedication. Again, immediately
after his account of the Transfiguration, St. Luke begins his
account of Christ's going up to suffer, 'when the days of His
ascension were being fulfilled' (Luke ix. 51) ; and Jesus Himself
said that His time to go up (to suffer) was not come at the previous
Feast of Tabernacles (John vii. 6), but connects the Transfiguration with predictions of His sufferings both before and after it.
A third argument is that there was a third Epiphany or manifestation of God's glory at the Transfiguration ; and if, as we
believe, the Transfiguration took place about the beginning of the
fourth year, all three Epiphanies or Inaugurations occurred at the
same season.[1]

THE PLACE BEYOND JORDAN, to which Jesus went away back
again (πάλιν), and where He abode after the Feast of Dedication,
was, perhaps, a district. It was the place where John was first
baptising. Now John is said to have come to all the country
adjoining (περίχωρος) the Jordan (Luke iii. 3 ; cp. Matt. iii. 5),
and to have preached first in the desert of Judea (Matt. iii. 1).
To determine where this desert was, it is to be remembered that
in Matt xix. 1, Jesus is said to have left Galilee and come into the
confines of 'Judea beyond Jordan,' that is, into Gaulonitis (mod.
Jolan) and Batanea, called also Basanitis, which seems to be the
old name Bashan in a Greek form. Now Josephus ('Wars,' iii. 3, 5)
assigns these provinces to Judea. St. John again represents John
the Baptist as first appearing in Bethany beyond Jordan. Now
this word Bethany appears to be the same as Batanea, or
Basanitis, or Bashan, for we find it reappearing in various
names of the districts of Bashan in modern times. The east of
Bashan still retains the name of El-Bethaniyeh. El-Batiheh is a

---

[1] 'The Early Christian expositors represented the Transfiguration as the
foreshadowing of the fulfilment of the promise, when Christ comes to take to
Himself His great power and reign in majesty' (Trench). This representation
exactly corresponds with that here given, where it introduces the fourth or
culminating year of Christ's ministry, as His birth and first year's ministry
were also introduced by Epiphanies. The scope of the narrative is not against
this. Andrews has no such reason for placing (in his new edition) the Transfiguration immediately after the Feast of Tabernacles. In the interval before
the Feast of Dedication he also places the payment of the Temple dues, the
Mission of the Seventy, and other events recorded in Luke ix. 51–xiii. 35.
He places Martha's supper on the way to the Feast of Dedication, but it fits
into the system here given if it occurred at the raising of Lazarus.

strip of fertile and well-watered country on the east of the Jordan, where it enters the Sea of Galilee ; and in the northern part of this strip travellers found ruins of a place called Tell-Anihje, which, by substituting Beth for the Arabic Tell, becomes Bethanihye (see Caspari, pp. 92, 93). This might justify Lightfoot's idea that Bethany was between Lake Merom and the Sea of Galilee, especially as John was probably not far from Bethsaida (John i. 28, 44). The name seems to occur again in El-Bothin, the modern name of a district of Decapolis, round the Grecianised Pella (the Batneh of the Talmud, Caspari, p. 104), where there was much water. The ancient Bashan probably extended from the Jabbok (Jarmuk ?) to Hermon ; and we may safely conclude that Bethany beyond Jordan, or the place where John first baptised, was some place or district not far from the Jordan, and north of the Jabbok. It may be another form of Beth-oniyeh, that is, a house of shipping, or a house of passage (Bethabara), or ford. But whether it derived its name from this or from Bashan, it was on the way from Jerusalem to Cæsarea Philippi (the modern Banias), which was in the northern part of Bashan, at the base of Mount Hermon, and not far from the sources of the Jordan.

THE TRANSFIGURATION took place when Jesus had come into the parts (Matt. xvi. 13) or villages (Mark viii. 27) of Cæsarea Philippi.[1]   These parts or districts may have been the parts of Bashan of which Cæsarea Philippi was the capital, the Tetrarchy of Philip. When Jesus left the Feast of Dedication, He went back again ($\pi\acute{a}\lambda\iota\nu$) to the place where John first baptised, that is, to some district beyond Jordan, either in Philip's territories, the capital of which was Cæsarea Philippi, or on the way to it. It was on some mountain in this district, probably on one of the spurs of the lofty Hermon, that Jesus was transfigured. After the Transfiguration Jesus abode some time in Galilee (Mark xvii. 22) ; they 'passed along' ($\pi\alpha\rho\epsilon\pi\sigma\rho\epsilon\acute{u}\sigma\nu\tau\sigma$) through it (Mark ix. 30), by which expression we may understand 'a border-journey by the course of the Jordan' (McClellan, p. 578a).

THE LAST JOURNEY to suffer at Jerusalem has for its starting point the Mount of Transfiguration, not Capernaum. The way

---

[1] According to Matthew and Mark, Jesus ascended the Mount of Trans-figuration six days after Peter's confession. He probably did so at sunset, after six entire days, and was transfigured at early dawn (Andrews). Next day He descended, and thus the whole period from the confession to the Transfiguration was about a week, or, as St. Luke calls it, eight days. Josephus also speaks of a week as eight days. David, he says, 'ordained that each course of the priests should minister to God eight days from Sabbath to Sabbath' (*Ant.* vii. 14, 7). People still speak in this way.

led through Capernaum. On the way thither, a reasoning arose among the disciples who should be greatest in the kingdom of heaven ; but it was not till they came to Capernaum, and, according to St. Matthew's order, not till the Temple tribute had been paid, that Jesus inquired of them what the subject of their reasoning had been,[1] and rebuked their ambitious spirit, at the same time warning them against intolerance. The Temple tribute was a half-shekel, equal to two Roman denarii, or two drachmas, each drachma being nominally about $7\frac{1}{2}d.$ or $8\frac{1}{2}d.$ (R.V.) of our money, but in reality a good day's wages. This heavy tax was religiously paid by every Jew, whether in Palestine or abroad. In Palestine the collection began on the 1st of Adar, and on the 15th of Adar (about March 9), the official 'money-changers' or collectors who supplied shekels for ordinary coins, set up their booths or tables in each country town and demanded the tribute. After the 25th pledges were taken from those who had not paid it. The 15th of Adar was exactly a month before the Passover. Now there is every reason to believe that the Temple tribute for Jesus and Peter (a stater) was paid about the beginning of March. Those who suppose that it was paid by Jesus in the previous September as the arrears of the previous year, have probably been led to this supposition by a mistake as to St. Luke's order. On first reading his account it might appear that he places the refusal of the Samaritans to receive Jesus, the account of the aspirants, and the Mission and the return of the Seventy disciples after Christ's rebuke at Capernaum, which followed the payment of the Temple tribute. But in the three weeks that intervened between the payment of the Temple dues about the 15th of Adar (March 9) and Christ's arrival at Bethany, six days before the Passover, there is not time for the numerous visits to cities and places for which the Mission of the Seventy was preparatory (Luke x. 1), and also for Christ's visit to Bethany, when Lazarus was raised, the sojourn at Ephraim, and the final journey from Ephraim, probably through Perea. It is therefore important to notice that, although St. Luke certainly places the refusal of the Samaritans to receive Jesus, the coming of the aspirants, and the Mission of the Seventy after the reasoning which arose about pre-eminence, he does not necessarily mean that these events followed Christ's rebuke at Capernaum. Immediately after his account of the Transfiguration, the cure of the epileptic boy, and Christ's predictions of His death, St. Luke tells us of the reasoning of the disciples about pre-eminence. It probably began soon

---

[1] They at first made no answer (Mark ix. 33), and afterwards referred the question in dispute to Jesus (Matt. xviii. 1).

after the Transfiguration, and in connection with the privilege given to Peter, James, and John, as witnesses of that event. It was, in all likelihood, not one dispute, but an unsettled question, coming up again and again when the disciples were not in the immediate presence of Jesus. St. Luke says nothing about their coming to Capernaum, and after having mentioned the reasoning, he naturally connects the rebuke of Jesus with it, although that rebuke did not take place till some weeks after the reasoning began, and, if St. Matthew's order be followed, not till the Temple dues were paid. Any historian, after beginning such a short piece of history, consisting of two parts separated by an interval of time, will naturally and properly join the two parts together. St. Mark also joins them together ; but his method is to begin the account of the rebuke and then go back for an explanation (Mark ix. 33, 34). Another parallel instance of a similar connecting of two parts of an event, though separated by an interval of time, occurs in the subsequent healing of Blind Bartimæus. It was at the entrance of Jericho that, according to St. Luke (xviii. 35), the noise of the crowd accompanying Jesus first attracted the attention of Bartimæus as he sat begging. But as he was inquiring the company would be going away, and he would probably have to be told more about Jesus before he made so urgent an appeal for aid. Accordingly, we are told by St. Matthew (xx. 29), and St. Mark (x. 46), that Blind Bartimæus was healed as Jesus went out of Jericho. Bartimæus, hearing about the extraordinary works of Jesus, and knowing that He was going to the feast, waited by the side of the way leading to Jerusalem till Jesus left the house of Zacchæus and went out of Jericho. He is not now represented by these two Evangelists as begging or inquiring what the noise of the crowd meant. If historians did not connect such parts of a narrative together, their narratives would appear like disconnected annals and lose effect. We conclude that, although St. Luke mentions Christ's rebuke of ambition and intolerance immediately after His account of the reasoning about pre-eminence, yet that this rebuke followed some events which he next mentions—namely, the refusal of the Samaritans to allow Christ to go towards Jerusalem, the coming of the aspirants, the Mission of the Seventy, and perhaps the interview with the young lawyer. These events, therefore, took place in the two months which intervened between the Transfiguration and the payment of the Temple dues on the 15th of Adar (about March 9).[1] The Mission of the Seventy at the

---

[1] When St. Luke says that the Mission of the Seventy took place ' after these things ' (Luke x. 1), it is impossible to take this statement in any other

beginning of the fourth year was 'to be before the face' of Jesus, as He visited the different cities and places (Luke x. 1), and thus corresponded with the Mission of the Apostles at the beginning of the third year. The analogy also appears in the woes pronounced against impenitent cities at the time of both Missions.

DURING THE THREE WEEKS which followed the payment of the Temple dues and preceded the Passion week, Jesus went to Bethany and raised Lazarus from the dead. This corresponds with St. Luke's account of Martha's entertainment (Luke x. 38). The Ephraim at which He tarried or abode after this was, in all probability, a place in the north of Judea, on the borders of Samaria, about 20 Roman miles (according to Jerome) from Jerusalem, mentioned along with Bethel in 2 Chron. xiii. 19, and by Josephus ('Wars,' iv. 9, 9). In order to join the company of Galileans going to the Passover Jesus probably went northwards through the midst of Samaria and then eastward through the borderland or adjoining part of Galilee (Andrews), crossing into Perea by the ford at Bethshean; and there is every reason to believe that St. Luke speaks of this journey (Luke xvii. 11), as he puts Samaria before Galilee.[1] The Samaritans would not hinder Jesus from going away from Jerusalem.

⁑ THE ACCOUNTS OF THE PASSION WEEK require that a few expressions susceptible of a double meaning should be defined. Jesus arrived in Bethany six days before the Passover (John xii. 1). (1) As Jesus would not travel on the Jewish Sabbath, the question has arisen whether He arrived on the Friday afternoon, which is exactly six days before the following Thursday afternoon, when

sense than that of chronological sequence. McClellan is not justified in saying (p. 450) that this only means after the Mission of the Apostles, and not after the numerous events which St. Luke places between the two Missions. But we are justified in omitting from 'these things' the rebuke of Jesus at Capernaum, seeing that St. Luke merely attached this to his account of the disputed question of pre-eminence, as Mark also connects the two parts of the incident, telling us that they occurred at different times. Instead of putting the Mission of the Seventy before the payment of the Temple tribute, Greswell and others, who abide by St. Luke's chronology, put back this payment by Jesus into the preceding year, and represent it as the payment of the previous year's arrears. This gives time for Christ's apparently numerous visits after this Mission, but the supposition of arrears is unnatural, and also unlikely. As the Transfiguration is placed by St. Luke before this Mission, the same difficulty has probably led so many harmonists to assign too early a date also to the Transfiguration.

[1] The Greek expression translated 'through the midst of Samaria and Galilee' is by some translated 'through the borderland of (between) Samaria and Galilee,' and this translation would be advisable, if it were not probable that Jesus made this journey 'with His face' away from Jerusalem.

the Paschal lambs were sacrificed, or whether He spent the Sabbath in the house of Zacchæus, arriving in Bethany on our Sunday, and making His triumphal entry into Jerusalem, not on Palm Sunday, but on the following Monday. This last supposition would imply that the Paschal lambs were killed on Friday, and those who hold it think that Jesus Christ did not eat the Paschal lamb at all, but suffered at the time when it was being sacrificed. Against this theory we have already quoted the high authority of Irenæus (ii. 21, 3) ; and though this arrangement of events is followed by a few learned men,[1] the other is much preferable, or at all events generally received. (2) The Thursday on which the Paschal lambs were killed is called the first day of Unleavened Bread (Matt. xxvi. 17 ; Mark xvi. 12 ; Luke xxii. 7), because all the old leaven was on that day carefully put out of the houses. In counting this day as the first day of the Feast, Josephus sometimes calls the Passover a Feast of eight days ('Ant.' ii. 15, 1). The Paschal lamb was eaten on the evening after the sun had gone down ; and (3) the morning that followed with the rest of the daytime was called the Feast (*chag*) or Festivity (*chagigah*)[2] in the Pentateuch (Lev. xxiii. 5, 6 ; Num. xxviii. 16, 17 ; cp. Deut. xvi. 2, 7), and by Josephus ('Ant.' iii. 10, 5).

[1] According to our reckoning, Jesus entered on His public ministry in January, A.U.C. 780, and His last Passover, being in the fourth year after this, was in A.U.C. 783. It began at sunset between Nisan 14 and Nisan 15 at full moon. Now the question is, whether the Friday on which Jesus was crucified was Nisan 14, when the Paschal lambs were killed, or Nisan 15, the Chagigah. This question resolves itself into another—namely, whether the month Nisan began on Thursday or Friday at sunset. Dr. Salmon has calculated that the moon was in conjunction with the sun about 8 o'clock on the Wednesday preceding; and, if we assume this to be accurate, the question comes to be whether the new moon *could* have been seen on the following Thursday. The new moon would set about 7 o'clock or shortly after ; and this gives only twenty-three hours of an interval. Skilled observers were on the watch ; and instances are given by Caspari (pp. 14, 15) and Andrews, (new ed. p. 41), which prove that the moon has been seen by Kepler, Americus, and the Jews less than twenty hours after conjunction. If the moon was not visible on the evening after the 29th day of the month, the month was, without more observation, declared to be one of thirty days and a new month begun. According to Dr. Salmon's calculations, the *only* other year about this time when the new moon could have been first seen on Thursday evening was the year A.U.C. 787 ; and this would go to prove the common era of Christ's birth.

[2] The Feast (of the Passover) sometimes means all the Passover and sometimes the Chagigah, or festal day which followed the eating of the Paschal lamb. When John says (xiii. 1) that before the Feast Jesus knew that He would suffer death at the Feast, and that knowing this, immediately before or about the time of the eating of the lamb, He gave His disciples a last proof of His love by washing their feet, John may either mean the Chagigah or the

This Chagigah was part of the Passover (2 Chron. xxxv. 6–14 ; Deut. xvi. 2–17) ; it was this Passover, or part of the Passover, that the Jews wished to eat, and therefore did not enter the Roman Prætorium (John xviii. 28). The trials of Jesus before Herod and Pilate ended (4) about the sixth hour (John xix. 14). This must have been according to the civil reckoning of the Romans, which John elsewhere follows (John iv. 6, 52 ; cp. Gen. xxiv. 11), and we may reasonably suppose that John means some time between 6 and 7 A.M. Now the formal trial before the Jewish council took place 'as soon as it was day'—that is, as soon as the watchman on the Temple top proclaimed the first streaks of dawn (Edersheim, vol. i. p. 244), and at this season of the year dawn might be there discernible about 4.50 A.M. Nearly two hours would thus be allowed for the trials, and perhaps the scourging ; and this is sufficient.[1] (5) The 'Preparation of the Passover' spoken of in John xix. 14, and 'the Preparation' spoken of elsewhere (John xix. 31, 42 ; Luke xxiii. 54, &c.) was not the first day of Unleavened Bread, but the Passover Friday—the Friday of the Passover week ; for St. Luke says distinctly that it was the Preparation, and the Sabbath 'drew on' (ἐπέφωσκε, Luke xxiii. 54), and Josephus ('Ant.' xvi. 6, 2) uses the word 'Preparation' in the sense of Friday.[2] (6) The expression 'drew on,' which

[1] whole Passover.   When Judas went out during the Paschal supper (John xiii. 29), some of the apostles thought that he was sent to buy something for the Feast ; and this may mean something required at once for the Supper, or something for the Chagigah after the morning came.

[1] Another suggestion may be ventured.   In the Alexandrine Codex, now in the British Museum, the passage reads **ⲰⲢⲀⲎⲰⲤⲈⲔⲦⲎ.** The word HN is written Ĥ, because in the Codex it stands at the end of the line. Now, if the original words in St. John's autograph were these, and if we suppose that the stroke above H was the accent, or breathing, or put in as if to end H *was*, the words might be read ἅρα ἦως ἕκτη, that is, the daytime was the sixth morning (of the week).   The words would, therefore, contain an explanation of the Friday Preparation, which was the sixth day of the week, the days being called first, second, third, &c. (Iren. v. 23, 2).   It is quite common in the New Testament to have a word occurring only once, and this word ἦως occurs in an adjectival form in the Septuagint ἡ ἑωθινὴ φυλακή, the morning watch.   There were two mornings in the Hebrew way of speaking.   The first 'dawn of day,' would be the Greek ὄρθρος, and the second morning called *boker*, the time before 9 A.M. (see Smith's *Dict. of the Bible*, under *day*) would rather in Greek be ἦως.   If this were the proper reading, St. John merely asserted that Pilate pronounced sentence in the morning between sunrise and the forenoon (ab. 9 A.M.) of the sixth day. The Greek text of the passage is in other respects dubious, some MSS. inserting δὲ and others putting ὡσεὶ for ὡς.

[2] The chief reason for the Preparation before the weekly Sabbaths was because it was not allowed to prepare food on them ; whereas on feasts

has just been quoted, means generally any time from the previous eve till dawn of day. In Matt. xxviii. 1 the same Greek word is translated 'as it began to dawn' (towards the first day of the week). The word might be translated 'on the eve' of the first day of the week, that is in 'the late evening' (ὀψέ) of or after the Sabbath. This would imply that the two Marys visited the sepulchre on Saturday after sunset, when they had completed their purchase of spices (Mark xvi. 1). But they certainly came very early next morning ; and if St. Matthew speaks of this, what follows shows how in Hebraistic Greek *and* does not necessarily imply sequence. We should have to translate 'And behold, there had been a great earthquake.' Hebrew has no pluperfect. (7) The high (great) day during which Jesus was in the grave was the second day of Passover, called 'high' or 'great' because it was the day when the first of the harvest was waved before the Lord, and because it was a day of solemn convocation in the Temple courts.

Synoptical Table of the Fourth Year.
The days of Christ's last ascent till Passion Week.

	Matt.	Mark	Luke	John
On the way to Cæsarea Philippi, Jesus	xvi.	viii.	ix.	
was confessed by Peter to be God's Son ;	13–20	27–30	18–21	
but Peter could not understand how	xvi.	viii.	ix.	
God's Son was to be killed and raised again.	21–28	31–38	22–27	
Early in January, A.D. 30, Jesus was	xvii.	ix.	ix.	
transfigured, probably on Mount Hermon.	1–13.	1–13	28–36	
(This is my beloved Son, mine elect, &c.)				
On descending the mountain, He	xvii.	ix.	ix.	
healed the deaf-mute epileptic boy, and	14–23	14–32	37–45	
foretold His death and resurrection.				
A reasoning arose among the disciples		ix.	ix.	
which of them should be greatest.		34	46	
St. Luke's peculiar section begins with			ix.	
Christ's setting His face to go to Jeru-salem, 'as the days of His ascension were being fulfilled.'			51	
The Samaritans, in answer to Christ's			ix.	
messengers, refused Him a passage.			52–56	
Some aspirants were admonished what	cp. viii.		ix.	
they must turn their backs upon.	19–22		57–62	

reckoned as Sabbaths only servile work was forbidden. This accounts for the word Preparation becoming a definite synonym for Friday, while the previous days of the week were called first, second, third, &c.

	Matt.	Mark	Luke	John
The Mission of the Seventy, like that of the Apostles, was early in the year.			x. 1–24	
In answer to a young lawyer's question, ' Who is my neighbour ?' the Parable of the Good Samaritan was spoken.			x. 25–37	
Jesus now reached Capernaum, where He paid the Temple dues about March 9, reproved the ambition of the disciples, setting before them a little child, and enjoined a forgiving spirit by the Parable of the Unmerciful Servant.	xvii. 24–27 xviii. 1–14 xviii. 15–35	ix. 33 ix. 33–50	ix. 47–50	
He now left Capernaum, possibly passing through between Samaria and Galilee ; and, reaching Perea, heard of the illness of Lazarus, to raise whom He went to Bethany.	xix. 1, 2	x. 1	x. 38	xi. 1–53
Here He was entertained by Martha who served ; Mary chose the better part.			x. 38–42	
After this He retired to Ephraim, and abode there, probably more than a week.				xi. 54–57
St. Luke's peculiar section contains recapitulatory parts and the following :—				
The Parables of the Importunate Friend and the Strong Man Armed.			xi. 1–26	
Who are the blessed ? One greater than Solomon and greater than Jonah.			xi. 27–32	
The light of the body must be open, and not obscurantist or malignant.			xi. 33–36	
Woes on the Pharisees and Lawyers. Beware of hypocrisy. Whom to fear.			xi. 37– xii. 12	
Beware of covetousness. The Rich Fool. Watch, for ye know not the hour.			xii. 13–50	
The tower in Siloam. The Cumbering Fig Tree. Woman healed on Sabbath.			xiii. 1–17	
Are there few that be saved ? Answer to Herod : ' Go and tell that fox.'			xiii. 22–35	
On Sabbath Jesus dined with a ruler of the Pharisees, healed the dropsy, reproved guests who chose the chief places, and described true hospitality.			xiv. 1–6 xiv. 7–14	
He then spoke the Parable of the Great Supper, and addressed the multitude about counting the cost.			xiv. 15–35	

	Matt.	Mark	Luke	John
The Parables of the Lost Sheep, the			xv.	
Lost Piece of Money, and the Prodigal			1-32	
Son, justified His receiving sinners.			.	
On the right use of Riches. The Un-			xvi.	
just Steward, who made wise provision.			1-18	
On the wrong use of Riches. Lazarus			xvi.	
and Dives are described in Hades, that			19-21	
is, before the judgment.				
On forgiving others, and deeming our-			xvii.	
selves to be unprofitable servants.			1-10	
Leaving Ephraim He passed through			xvii.	
Samaria and the Galilean border to join			11	
the company of Galilean pilgrims. He			xvii.	
then healed ten lepers, showed how			12-19	
the kingdom of God cometh not with			xvii.	
observation, here or there, and spoke			20-37	
the Parables of the Unjust Judge, the			xviii.	
Pharisee and the Publican.			1-14	
Crossing into Perea, He discoursed on	xix.	x.	xviii.	
Moses' law of divorce; bade them bring	1-12	1-12	15-17	
little children to Him, for the truth is	xix.	x.	xviii.	
committed to such; showed the rich	13-15	13-16	18-27	
young ruler how hard it was to cease	xix.	x.	xviii.	
from covetousness;[1] told what those	16-26	17-27	28-30	
leaving all to follow Him would have;	xix. 27	x.	xviii.	
and spoke the Parable of the Labourers.	xx. 16	28-31	31-34	
He then clearly foretold His passion,	xx.	x.		
and answered the request of James and	17-28	32-45		
John, made through their mother.				
Entering Jericho, He was heard pass-			xviii.	
ing by Bartimæus and lodged with			35-37	
Zacchæus, in whose house He spake the			xix.	
Parable of the Pounds. On leaving He			1-28	
was addressed by Bartimæus,[2] who, with	xx.	x.	xviii.	
a companion, received sight.	29-34	46-52	38-43	

[1] The Revisers have adopted a very questionable reading in Matt. xix. 17, on the authority of the manuscripts א, B, D, L, 1, and in spite of all the other manuscripts. But even if we follow this reading, Christ's full answer might have combined this reading with that given by St. Mark and St. Luke: 'Why askest thou me concerning that which is good? or why callest thou me good? There is none good but one, that is God.'

[2] According to Bengel, Stier, Trench, Ellicott and MacClellan, Bartimæus heard the company of Jesus passing as they entered Jericho, but was not then healed; he then joined himself to another blind man and waited for Jesus as

	Matt.	Mark	Luke	John
Six days before the Passover, and therefore on Friday, He arrived in Bethany.[1]				xi. 55 xii. 1
Next day, at supper, He was anointed, in Simon the Leper's house, by Mary.	xxvi. 6–13	xiv. 3–9		xii. 2–8

CHRIST'S PASSION WEEK, RESURREC-
TION AND ASCENSION.

On Palm Sunday, the day for selecting the Paschal Lamb, Jesus entered Jeru- salem as the son of David and King.[2]	xxi. 1–17	xi. 1–11	xix. 29–44	xii. 12–19
On Monday He cursed the fig-tree, cleansed the Temple, and healed the blind and lame in it.	xxi. 18, 19	xi. 12–19	xix. 45–48	
On Tuesday He spoke about the with- ered fig-tree and the children's hosannahs, answered a question about His authority by a counter question about John and by Parables of the Two Sons, the Wicked Husbandmen, and the King's Marriage Feast and the Wedding Garment.	xxi. 20–22 xxi. 23–46 xxi. 1–14	xi. 20–26 xi. 27–33 xii. 1–12	xx. 1–8 xx. 9–19	

He left Jericho next morning, when both were healed ; but St. Luke relates both parts of the incident together, in order not to break the continuity of his narrative. As Jesus said to Zacchæus, ' To-day I must abide in thy house,' and as 'they murmured that He had gone to lodge (καταλῦσαι) with a man that was a sinner,' it follows that Jesus passed the night in the house of Zacchæus.

[1] The conjunction *and* does not always denote chronological or immediate sequence. The Synoptists omitted all mention of Christ's visit to Bethany before His Triumphal entry into Jerusalem, and therefore they delay giving us an account of the anointing till they have given the discourse on the Mount of Olives. When Mark says that 'after two days was the Feast of the Passover' (xiv. 10) he is giving the date of the conclusion of this discourse, and of the active steps taken against Jesus. When St. Matthew and St. Mark connect with this the account of the anointing by means of *and*, the Hebrew and Hellenistic style does not imply that this anointing followed the discourse or the treachery of Judas, though it served to account for it. The widow's answer to David was an instance : ' I am a widow woman of Tekoa and my husband died.' The Hebrew wants the pluperfect, and when the speaker's mind recurs to a previous event, it may be simply connected with *and—e.g.* Gen. ii. 19 ; xii. 1.

[2] The disciples brought the ass and the colt to Jesus and placed their garments upon them ; and Jesus sat upon them (Matt. xxi. 7). It is not necessary to interpret this as meaning that Jesus sat upon the garments. If He sat upon the colt only (John xii. 14), He sat upon the animals. A man may be said to sit upon the chairs of a room ; but this does not mean that he must needs be seated upon all of them. We must allow to language its legitimate range.

	Matt.	Mark	Luke	John
He next answered questions about	xxii.	xii.	xx.	
tribute to Cæsar, about the resurrection	15-33	13-27	20-40	
of the dead, and about the great com-	xxii.	xii.		
mandment of the Law (Deut. v. 6, and	34-40	28-34		
Lev. xix. 18).				

He then asked His questioners how xxii. xii. xx.
David's son could be David's Lord (Ps. cx.); 41-46 35-37 41-44
denounced the hypocrisy, blind guidance xxiii. xii. xx.
and venom of Scribes and Pharisees; 1-39 38-40 45-47
and, sitting down over against the treasury, xii. xxi.
praised the widow's mite. 41-44 1-4.

Here he probably was told of Greeks xii.
seeking Him, and the voice came from 20-29
heaven. His discourse indicated that xii.
men would be judged by His word, ac- 30-50
cording as they kept or disregarded it.

Leaving the Temple He predicted its xxiv. xiii. xxi.
destruction, discoursed on the signs of 1-57 1-37 5-38
His coming, the end of the age, and the xxv.
judgment, speaking Parables of the Ten 1-46
Virgins, Talents, and Sheep and Goats.

On Wednesday the chief priests and xxvi. xiv. xxii.
Scribes bargained with Judas purposing 14-16 1, 10, 11 1-6
since the anointing to betray Jesus.

On Thursday Peter and John were xxvi. xxiv. xxii.
sent to make ready the Passover. In the 17-19 12-16 7-13
evening, after rebuking a contention xxvi. xiv. xxii. xiii.
about precedence, Jesus washed His 20 17 24 2-20
disciples' feet. (-)30

He then ate the Passover; and xxvi. xiv. xxii. xiii.
during it pointed out the traitor Judas 21-25 18-21 14-23 21-
by a sop. 32

After this He instituted the Eucharist, xxvi. xiv. xxii.
the cup of blessing being the third in 26-29 22-25 19, 20
the old ritual. (1 Cor. xi. 23-35).

He then announced His near separa- xxii. xiii.
tion, enjoined love and foretold Peter's 22-36 33-38
denials, promised the Spirit as another xiv.
Comforter, and enjoined abidance in His 1-31
teaching.[1]

---

[1] His answer to Jude and previous words indicate the two great means of grace—the keeping or studying of His sayings, and the keeping of His commandments or proper conduct. Man's character, according to the laws of

	Matt.	Mark	Luke	John
The Hallel (Ps. cxv.–cxviii.) was then	xxvi.	xiv.		xiv.
sung; and they left the supper room.	30	26		31
When arising to go or on the way to				xv.
the Mount of Olives He concluded His				xvi.
farewell discourse, spoke the intercessory	xxvi.	xiv.	xxii.	xviii.
prayer, and again predicted the apostles'	31–35	27–31	39	
desertion.				
The agony in Gethsemane, the angel's	xxvi.	xiv.	xxii.	
appearance, the sweat as of great drops	36–46	32–42	40–46	
of blood followed; then, after mid-	xxvi.	xiv.	xxii.	xviii.
night, the betrayal of Judas, the arrest	47–56	43–52	46–53	2–11
of Jesus, and the flight of the apostles.				
Jesus was led a prisoner first before				xvii
Annas, the leader of the Sanhedrim; and				12–14
then tried informally before Caiaphas,[1]	xxvi.	xiv.	xxii.	xviii.
in whose house before cock-crowing	57–75	53–72	54–65	15–27
Peter denied him thrice.[2]				
When dawn was announced from	xxvii.	xv.	xxii.	
	1	41	66–71	

growth, is affected both by what he knows or thinks about, and also by what he practises. We have, it is true, nothing of our own to give to God, nor does He Himself need anything from us. Works of merit are excluded, but not works of means, for men's characters depend greatly on their actions. Works of mercy bless the giver as well as the receiver.

[1] The Sanhedrim would not be idle till daybreak. Jesus was probably first examined by Annas; but John does not tell us where. He was then informally tried during night in the house of Caiaphas (Matthew and Mark); and then formally tried when the legal time came at the first break of day (Luke).

[2] Peter's denials may be thus harmonised. First, the maid who kept the door of the porch leading into the hall or open court of the high priest's house, saw Peter sitting and (sometimes) standing in the light of the fire, and said to him, 'Thou also wert with Jesus of Nazareth; art thou one of His disciples?' He answered: 'I am not; I know not him or what thou art speaking about.' He then went into the porch and the cock crew. After this, another maidservant saw him and said to them that stood by, 'This is one of them.' Another man then said to him, 'Thou also art one of them.' One or more of the bystanders asked him, 'Art thou also one of His disciples?' On this he again denied with an oath, saying, 'Man, I am not; I know not the man.' About an hour afterwards a certain man, among other bystanders, said to him, 'Of a truth thou art one of them, for thou art a Galilean, and thy speech agreeing thereto bewrayeth thee.' Also a kinsman of Malchus said to him, 'Did I not see thee with Him in the garden?' Then began he to curse and to swear, saying to one, 'Man, I know not what thou sayest,' and to the bystanders, 'I know not the man of whom you speak.' And while he yet spake the cock crew the second time. St. Mark speaks of the cock crowing twice; but St. Matthew merely says that before cock-crowing, that is, before the fourth watch of the night, Peter was to deny his Master thrice.

	Matt.	Mark	Luke	John

the Temple top (ab. 4.50 A.M.), He was
tried formally by the Sanhedrim.

The Temple door being then opened, xxvii.   Acts i.
Judas, in despair, cast the blood-money 3–10   18–19
into the sanctuary, and hanged himself.[1]
At early dawn (5 A.M.), Jesus was xxvii. xv. xxiii. xviii.
led before Pilate, who found Him in- 2, 11, 1–5   1–4 28–38
nocent; but hearing He was of Galilee, 14
Pilate sent Him to Herod, who mocked xxiii.
Him, and sent him back. 5–12

Pilate then sought to release Jesus xxviii. xv. xxiii. xviii.
according to a custom at the Feast; but 15–25 6–14 13–23 39–
the Jews preferred Barabbas.   40
Pilate now sought to content the Jews   xix.
by scourging Jesus (Behold the Man!),   1–5
but fearing to be reported to Tiberius, xxvii. xv. xxiii. xix.
delivered Him to be crucified. 26–33 15–22 24–32 6–16
At 9 A.M. Jesus was crucified, refus- xxvii. xv. xxiii. xix.
ing the drugged wine.[2] His first words 34–38 23–28 33, 34 17–
from the Cross were, 'Father, forgive   24
them, for they know not what they do.'
The priests, the people, the soldiers, xxvii. xv. xxiii.
and at least one of the two malefactors 39–44 29–32 35–38
crucified with Him, railed at Him.[3] To

[1] St. Peter, in speaking of the fall of Judas from the high place or estate of apostleship, contrasted with it the place or estate which he 'got for himself' with the wages of iniquity (Acts i. 18). The Greek word (ἐκτήσατο) means 'got' or 'obtained' (R.V.), and does not necessarily imply that Judas himself purchased the Field of Blood (Aceldama), which perpetuated the memory of his treachery. 'Falling down headlong, he burst in the midst, and all his bowels gushed out.' The meaning clearly is that he burst in the midst of his person; the same word (μέσος), translated 'in the midst,' occurs in this sense in Luke xxiii. 45. The quotation from Jeremiah the prophet (Matt. xxvii. 9, 10) is not among Jeremiah's written words, as now recorded; but the Jews had other traditions of the sayings of their great prophets, besides those in our written Scriptures. The words are not exactly those of Zechariah (xi. 12, 13), who adapted them to his own context.

[2] It is quite immaterial whether we read *wine* in Matt. xxvii. 34, *vinegar*. We know, from Mark xv. 24, that wine was first offered to Jesus mingled with drugs to stupefy and allay pain. This Jesus refused. The word translated vinegar (Gk. ὄξος, Heb. *chomets*, Lat. acetum, was often applied to the poor wine of the country (cp. Fr. *vin aigre*).

[3] St. Matthew does not mention this incident of the repentant thief, but enumerates the thieves as among the classes who reviled Christ on the cross. It is unnecessary to suppose that the repentant thief reviled Christ before He repented, though he may have done so. St. Matthew is speaking of classes of men.

	Matt.	Mark	Luke	John
the repentant malefactor He said, 'To-day thou shalt be with me in Paradise.'			xxiii. 39-43	
To John, standing by, Jesus commended His mother, and said, 'Behold thy mother,' 'Woman, behold thy son.'				xix. 25-27
The supernatural darkness began at noon, and lasted three hours (Eli, Eli).	xxvii. 45-47	xv. 33-35	xxiii. 44-49	
Jesus then said, 'I thirst,' and, receiving vinegar, cried, 'It is finished,' and with the words, 'Father, into Thy hands I commit my Spirit,' bowed His head and died. The centurion and the women looked on. To make sure He was dead, a soldier pierced His side, whence came blood and water.[1] Before sunset, He was buried by Joseph and Nicodemus.	xxvii. 48-56 57-61	xv. 36-41 42-47	xxiii. 50-55	xix. 28-30 xix. 31-37 xix. 38-7 42
On the second day of the Passover, being this year Sabbath, Jesus was in the grave, which was sealed, with a guard set to prevent the removal of the body.	xxvii. 62-66		xxiii. 56	
After Sabbath, on Sunday eve, the two Marys bought spices and perhaps visited the sepulchre.	xxviii. 1	xvi. 1		
There was a great earthquake; an angel descended and rolled the stone from the tomb, when Jesus rose again.	xxviii. 2-4			
The women, coming early to the sepulchre to embalm Jesus, saw the stone removed, and the grave empty.		xvi. 2-4	xxiv. 1-3	
Mary Magdalene either came first, or left the others to tell Peter and John, who found it so. Returning she saw Jesus.		xvi. 9-11		xx. 1-18
When she was away the other women saw a vision of angels, and went to report; returning they met Jesus.	xxviii. 5-10	xvi. 5-8	xxiv. 4-12	
Some of the terrified guards reported	xxviii. 11-15			

[1] The Roman Centurion's words in full were: 'Truly this was a righteous man, the (a) Son of God' (Luke xxiii. 47; Matt. xxviii. 54). There is a latent significance (cp. 1 John v. 6) in the water and the blood, which flowed from Christ's side. Water is often a type of the Word, and the blood of the Sacrifice was the Life. God's two Hands, according to Irenæus, are the Word and Spirit (iv. 20, 1; v. 1, 3; v. 6, 1).

Matt. Mark Luke John

what had happened, but were bribed to
say Jesus was stolen.

Jesus next appeared to Cleopas and   xvi. xxiv.
another disciple, perhaps Luke (?), going   12, 13 13-35
to Emmaus in the afternoon.

The same evening He was seen by 1 Cor. xvi. xxiv. xx.
Peter. He then appeared to the apostles, xv.   14 36-43 19-
declaring their mission, and breathing on 4, 5   23
them as future ministers of His grace.

A week later he again appeared to   xx.
them when Thomas was present, and   24-31
convinced him (My Lord and my God).

After this He appeared to seven dis-   xxi.
ciples as they were fishing at the Lake of   1-14
Galilee ; and, after a second miraculous   xxi.
draught of fishes, Peter received a pas-   15-25
toral charge. He was to die like Christ.

Jesus then appeared to five hundred xxviii.   1 Cor.
brethren, and probably in their presence 16-20   xv. 6
gave the apostles their commission.

He then appeared to James, the Lord's   xxiv. 1 Cor.
brother ; and finally, forty days after the   44-53 xv. 7
resurrection, He appeared to the apostles   xvi. Acts i.
at Jerusalem, led them out to Bethany,   19 3-11
and ascended to Heaven.

Christ's Appearances after His Ascension and Dispensational Developments.

AFTER the Ascension of Jesus Christ at Bethany, He reappeared
to St. Paul and St. John to initiate developments afterwards to be
worked out in the history of mankind. His fourth year's ministry
and subsequent appearances, reckoned as its sequel, form four
eras or developments connected with the witness and teaching of
Peter, James, Paul, and John, respectively ; and these developments, being the fulfilment of the days of ascension,[1] are analogous
to the periods of the three preceding years. St. Peter presents
himself in his epistles as an eye-witness of the Transfiguration and
similar facts, which he assures his readers were not cunningly
devised fables. In view of the sufferings and example of Jesus

---

[1] Forty days after Jesus Christ's birth, He was presented in the Temple ;
forty days after His baptism, He began His public ministry ; and forty days
after His resurrection, He appeared in His Church.

Christ, of the confirmation of the Word of prophecy, and of
Messianic expectation to be fulfilled, St. Peter exhorts them to
give earnest heed to this Word, to desire its sincere milk, to arm
themselves with a mind to endure as Christ did, to give diligence
to have their faith perfected. His epistles are thus a sequel to
St. Mark's Gospel, of which St. Peter was indirectly the author,
for all agree that this Gospel presents a rapid survey of the facts
of Christ's life, an eagle's (or bird's-) eye view of it. St. Peter's
Epistles lead on to that of James—the first Bishop of Jerusalem. If this was the James to whom Christ appeared immediately
before His ascension (1 Cor. xv. 7), we may regard this as a sort
of designation of him to this office. At Christ's last meeting with
His Apostles they asked Him about the kingdom He was to set
up. His reply indicated that the power of this kingdom was the
Holy Spirit to come at Pentecost, and that they were to be His
witnesses, that is, witnesses for His truth, for truth is the ruling
principle of His kingdom (cp. John xviii. 36-38). We have here
the first constitution of the Christian Church to be the guardian
and witness of the truth and the embodiment of the Spirit. It
was this kingdom of God's truth and the new mind implied in the
word ($\mu\epsilon\tau\acute{a}\nu o\iota a$) translated 'repentance,' that Jesus began to preach
at Capernaum at the commencement of His second year's ministry,
and the same feature occurs distinctly at the second era of each
year, from the Passover to Pentecost. So it was at the Passover
of the fourth year, at the commencement of the second stage of
that year, that Jesus rode into Jerusalem, publicly showing himself
as the Davidic King. In His trial before Pilate He represented
Himself as a King, but connected His kingdom with the truth to
which He was witnessing. After His passion, 'He spake the things
concerning the Kingdom of God.' On the Cross the title declared
Him to be King of the Jews. This aspect is that of Man reigning.
'Behold the Man,' said Pilate to the Jews. Now the same aspect
is presented in the Epistle of James. His themes are the royal
law (ii. 8), the perfect Image of Man (i. 23, R.V. marg.), the
wisdom that is from above (iii. 17), pure and undefiled religion
(i. 27), and the judgment on those who lead unworthy lives.
St. James's Epistle is thus a fitting sequel to St. Matthew's Gospel,
which begins with the royal pedigree of Jesus Christ and the
Magi's adoration of Him as King of the Jews, presenting Him as
the meek and lowly-minded pattern of men (xi. 30), yet as a King
sitting on the Mount to give His law, and on the throne of His
glory to judge the nations (Matt. xxv. 31, 32). The third era of
Gospel development is connected with the appearances of Jesus
Christ to Paul. The first appearance to him was on the way to

Damascus. Again, in Arabia, the country of the Levitical legislation, Paul received his instructions directly from Jesus Christ (Gal. i. 11–17). The third heaven, into which Paul was caught up, seems to connect itself with this third aspect. In the Temple he again saw Jesus in vision and was commissioned to go to the Gentiles (Acts xxii. 17–21); at Corinth (Acts xviii. 9), and on the way to Rome (Acts xxiii. 11) Paul had subsequent visions of Jesus Christ. Now St. Paul in his epistles deals largely with the sacrificial aspect of Christ (the ox-aspect of the Cherubim), and with the deep things of God. As Peter said, there are in Paul's epistles things hard to be understood or interpreted, which are a savour of life to some but may become a savour of death to perverters, if they interpret them in a sense contrary to the plain, uncontrovertible, first principles of all true religious belief. They present the wisdom of God hidden in a mystery, a discipline of enigmatic teaching analogous to that of the third year of Christ's ministry, and to the parabolic or covert aspect of the third stage of each year. The same aspect appears in the Gospel of his companion Luke, especially in the opening chapters and in the long parabolic section (ix. 51–xviii. 14) peculiar to him, which contains the most remarkable of all the Parables. This Parable shows how the Fatted Calf was killed because of the finding of the younger son (the Gentiles), while 'the gifts and calling of God' were secured to the elder (the Jews). The last appearance, or series of appearances, of Jesus Christ was to St. John in the Island of Patmos. The Epistles and Apocalyptic visions, which he was directed to write, follow up his Gospel, and complete the New Testament canon. John is called up into the heavenly presence of Him who is over all. Around His throne are twenty-four elders, seated also on thrones and clothed in white garments. Besides other imagery of the prophet Ezekiel, the four-faced Cherubim (Dispensational Aspects) appear in the midst of the throne and encircling it. He that sits upon the throne holds in His hand a roll written completely over; but no man is found worthy to open its seven seals, till the Lion of the Tribe of Judah prevails to do so. When this is announced by one of the elders, creation bursts forth in a new song of praise, declaring the Lamb that was slain worthy to receive power. At the opening of the first seal, One sitting on a white horse appears 'conquering and to conquer.' As David said, He comes in majesty, riding upon the Word or matter of ('al d'var) truth, meekness, and righteousness (Ps. xlv. 4). His approach is heralded by the first of the Cherubim, the Lion-faced, in a voice of thunder. Now the aspect which St. John (Boanerges) here represents, is that of conquest—of Jesus Christ subduing all things to Himself, whether in the natural use of things, in the full understanding of the mystery of God, or in raising men into the life and participation of God. The earth is lighted up when created things are devoted to man's service and God's glory; the mystery of God is unveiled, for John sees into the most holy place, where the ark of God is ; and man himself is to be perfected as the Temple of God, who is love and light and life. But in growing up to this perfected manhood, 'the steps to God are not few ;' and, in the working out of them, God has ever been a Trier of those upon whom He sends His goodness (Irenæus iii. 25 ; iv. 9). Thus the Book of Revelation is full of figurative descriptions of God's judgments. Created things, if misused, become a curse and a cause of contentious hatred, figured by a blood-red horse ; perversions of truth turn the lights of heaven to black darkness ; and, as the alternative of divine life, Hades and pale death follow in the train. The coming judgments are the parallels of the prizes. As men grow to maturity and enter upon the freedom which is proper to full growth, not to minors, they are more thoroughly tried (Iren. iv. 16, 5) ; but, if it be worthy, the working of liberty is 'greater and more glorious' (iv. 13, 2).

The fourfold division of the Gospel History is thus demonstrated by manifold recurrences. It is discernible (1) in the years of Jesus Christ's ministry, (2) in the divisions of the years, (3) in the characteristics of the Four Gospels, and (4) in the development of the New Testament Canon, being foreshadowed (5) in the Mosaic Feasts and (6) successive legislations.[1] Another remarkable confirmation of it appears in the order of the Cherubic aspects, which St. John gives apparently inverted (Rev. iv. 7), but which indicates an order of dispensational developments descending from the patriarchal or normal state, to re-ascend by inverted but analogous stages, till Paradise is regained in what is called the restitution of all things. 'At first,' says Irenæus, 'the Word

---

[1] First, we have the mission of Moses, beginning at the Burning Bush and including the mighty works done by his agency in Egypt, till the Exodus, when the Passover was instituted. Secondly, in the third month after they came out of Egypt, the Israelites reached Sinai (Ex. xix. 1). The Ten Commandments were thus given about Pentecost ; and at first God added no more (Deut. v. 22). But, thirdly, when the people by the idolatry of the golden calf showed themselves gross-minded, prone to idolatry, and in need of a sensuous and mediated discipline, they received for their good the elaborate ritual or priest code. Lastly, on the first day of the eleventh month of the fortieth year after leaving Egypt, and in the part of the Holy Land east of Jordan, Moses began to declare or expound (be'er) the law of Deuteronomy (Deut. i. 5) ; he recapitulates the past and indicates its fulfilment.

of God conversed with the patriarchs according to His divinity and glory' (κατὰ τὸ θεικὸν καὶ ἔνδοξον, aspect of power); but (secondly) He gave the priestly and liturgical dispensation (represented by the sacrificial ox) in the Law of Moses' (Iren. iii. 11, 8). Thirdly, there was a new epoch marked by the Kingdom of David, the Man after God's own heart, by the building of the Temple, and by the wisdom of Solomon. Fourthly, there was the dispensation, characterised by Hebrew prophecy, the Eagle aspect. This last descending aspect was the first of an ascending series leading back to the normal state.[1] Jesus Christ connected His ministry with the great Hebrew prophets, being baptised by John, the last of them ; and He began as 'a prophet mighty in word and deed before God and all the people' (Luke xxiv. 19). The kingly aspect, as has been said, was publicly entered on at His last Passover. The Christian Church, constituted at His Ascension and Pentecost, corresponded to Solomon's Temple ; and the first Christian literature after the New Testament presents little else than a collection of plain earnest preceptive wisdom. But the Roman world became nominally Christian —a mixed, semi-pagan multitude entered both then and when the Northern Barbarians overran the empire. Christianity adapted itself as a discipline suitable for these childish, gross-minded, but teachable peoples. This discipline combined a sensuous and enigmatic symbolism with an ascetic or negative tendency, shunning for a time the full legitimate use of things, till the multitudes should grow to a maturer state and be able to discern between the right use and the wrong. Neander[2] shows that the more earnest Christians in the early times preferred to cast away much that had been used by them when heathens in the service of sin, but which was capable of a nobler use ; they passed through this 'great straitenment' (cp. Rev. vii. 14 with Matt. vii. 14), lest there should be any false accommodation with evil ; and, both in the case of the individual and that of the general body, there was a temporary development repressing for a time the positive element of assimilation, by which alone Christianity could rule the world, appropriating all that properly belongs to man. This stage was analogous to the wilderness discipline under Moses, commemorated by the Feast of Tabernacles. The Church fled into the wilderness. But created things were to be emancipated in the

---

[1] Seven dispensational ages are thus grouped round a central one. Similar groupings occur in Rev. xiv. where six angels and their acts are grouped round the Son of Man, and in chap. xvii. 1 to xxii. 5, the central figure being in chap. xix. 11 (Kliefoth, Milligan).

[2] Neander's *Church History*, vol. i. pp. 361, 362, 382, 383 ; Bohn.

full growth of the sons of God. The institutions, social tone, and ruling influences of the world come to be on the right side ; and, in their dedication to God's service, the things of this life put on a new face, the houses of the City of God being all lighted up, as at the Feast of Dedication ; the patriarchal paradise of Genesis is regained. The 'great power and glory' of this 'manifestation' is no doubt connected with great agencies and ministrations, directed by a knowledge of God's ways, or the laws of things. But it is still possible to transgress these laws of God. The moral refuse is cast outside the City ; men see it preyed upon by the fire of unrest and the worm of corruption (Rev. xxi., xxii.).

ALTERNATIVES IN GOSPEL CHRONOLOGY.

When a science is in its infancy we have the mere details of observation without the general principles by which these are combined into a system, ' we know in part and we prophesy in part,' we have a piecemeal knowledge and expository scraps. But when the principles underlying these details are demonstrably established, the whole can be taught systematically, the observed phenomena and the equally certain explanations or demonstrated principles being commingled. This has been the case with astronomy since the days of Galileo, Kepler, and Newton ; and it may yet be the case with the teaching of Christianity. As a preliminary, we believe it has here been shown, with an amount of probability which is practically demonstration, that a clear system or methodic order underlies even the Gospel history ; but, in order to judge, readers require to balance the other alternatives.

I. The first point at which a few harmonists diverge brings into question the length of time which Jesus spent in Judea, baptising through His disciples, and the length of time occupied by His first circuit in Galilee. His baptising lasted till the end of John's baptising, for Jesus left Judea when He heard of John's imprisonment. Now, if John began to baptise about October 1, A.D. 26, or a little earlier, we may reasonably presume that his ministry would continue till December 1, A.D. 27, a period of little more than fourteen months ; and if Jesus began to baptise in May or June (A.D. 27), He surely did not change His entire plan of operations in twenty-seven days, as Greswell supposes, or in five weeks, as MacClellan supposes. Would His baptism acquire in this short time so ' all-pervading an influence ' that ' all men came to Him ' (John iv. 26) ? Or is it not more reasonable to assign five or six months to this baptismal mode of making disciples ? Again, if, as Greswell and MacClellan suppose, it was about the beginning of June that Jesus left Judea to settle in Galilee, how is the time to be filled up between this date and the plucking of the ears of corn by the disciples, which could not be before the beginning of the following April ? To fill up this long interval, Greswell and MacClellan suppose that Christ's first circuit in Galilee, after His settlement at Capernaum, lasted ten months. They justify this by the statement that Jesus ' went about all Galilee preaching ' (Matt. iv. 23, Mark i. 39). But this does not necessarily, or even naturally, mean that He visited every one of the 204 cities and villages in Galilee (see Josephus' ' Life,' 54). The probability is that the first circuit in Galilee lasted only during the first two or three months of the year A.D. 28 ; and this probability harmonises with the statement of Jesus, in passing through Samaria, that ' there are yet four months and then cometh the harvest.' A proverb would not have been so expressed—and *six* months intervened between seed time and harvest in Palestine. Men would still remember the Passover miracles (John iv. 45). This probability, therefore, becomes practically demonstration.

II. Wieseler, followed by Ellicott and others, would omit a year and crowd into the space of ten days or a fortnight all the events which occurred, according to St. Mark and St. Luke, between the plucking of the ears of corn by the disciples (not earlier than April, or Nisan 1) and the Passover (Nisan 14), when Jesus fed the Five Thousand (see p. 17). The reader will find these events in two of our synopses (from the top of p. 29 to the top of p. 38) extended, as in most harmonies, over an entire year; and an inspection of them proves Wieseler's alternative to be unreasonable.

III. If the reader agrees with Tatian, Chrysostom, Cyril, most of the Fathers, Calvin, Bengel, MacClellan, Friedlieb, Townsend, and Lewin in thinking that the feast spoken of in John v. was Pentecost, he will agree with us in thinking that Christ's presence at the Feast of Pentecost was in keeping with the entire second year's ministry. If, however, with Irenæus, Grotius, Lightfoot, Greswell, Robinson, Wordsworth, Archbishop Thomson, Andrews, and Kitto, he judges this feast to have been the Passover, his arrangement of the other events of the year will not thereby be altered. If it was on the second day of the Passover, and first day of counting to Pentecost, that the disciples plucked the ears of corn, he has only to suppose that they did so in the neighbourhood of Jerusalem. Nor would our general outline be affected, if the feast in question was the Feast of Purim, a merrymaking held on the 14th and 15th of Adar (March) to commemorate the deliverance of the Jews from the machinations of their enemy Haman. This opinion is supported by Kepler, Meyer, Lange, Tholuck, Wieseler, Ellicott, Tischendorf, Winer, and Farrar; but as the Feast of Purim was not one prescribed by the law of Moses, as it had very little of the religious element in it, and served rather to foster the national antipathies of the Jews, it seems highly improbable that an important chapter of Gospel history would be connected with it.

IV. The next alternative refers to the dates of the Transfiguration, the payment of the Temple dues, and the Mission of the Seventy. Greswell and Ellicott place the Transfiguration in the early summer of our third year (May 27), and the payment of the Temple dues a fortnight before the Feast of Tabernacles, and the Mission of the Seventy after this feast (Ellicott) or in the next February (Greswell). Andrews now places all three events between the Feast of Tabernacles and the Feast of Dedication. After mentioning the payment of the Temple dues, St. Matthew relates Christ's rebuke of the disciples' ambition as occurring 'in that hour'; and as St. Luke mentions the Mission of the Seventy after his account of this rebuke, these harmonists seem to have concluded that Christ did not pay the Temple dues at the regular time—that is, in the first two weeks of Adar, or March—probably because they suppose that there was not time for the Mission of the Seventy and the many visits of Jesus, which the Seventy heralded, in the three (or four) weeks before the Passover week. But as St. Luke would naturally finish at once his account of the reasoning about pre-eminence and the rebuke of it, his words do not imply that the Mission of the Seventy followed the rebuke at Capernaum, although he does mean that it followed the rising of the reasoning. By supposing that this Mission preceded the rebuke, we have abundance of time for it in the first months of the fourth year, after the Transfiguration, which we place at the commencement of this year. In this way, we are not obliged to put back the payment of the Temple dues or to make the harsh supposition that Jesus got into arrears of debt for dues payable before the preceding Passover, and had to be reminded of them. In this way, also, we do not, like Greswell and others, interpose a long interval between the Transfiguration scenes and the 'days of ascension,' when Jesus set His face steadfastly to go to Jerusalem, or, like others, suppose that this final journey began at the Feast of Tabernacles and was unnaturally long and circuitous.

V. An attempt has been made by the Rev. William Pound, in his ' Story of the Gospels' (Rivington, 1869), to show that each Evangelist is strictly exact in the chronological order of the events which he records, and that each intends to indicate this by his notes of time and particles of transition. To make this out, Mr. Pound supposes that Jesus carried on a fourfold system of teaching at different stages in different districts ; and that not only were there two great sermons, as Greswell also supposes, but that there were two healings of a servant of the same Roman Centurion, two similar messages from John the Baptist, two voyages from the same place to Gerasa or Gadara, with two similar healings of demoniacs and two destructions of swine, two raisings to life of a daughter of the Ruler of the Synagogue, two Missions of the Apostles, one to Judea and another to Galilee ! The particles (the Greek καί and δέ), by which St. Matthew introduces these accounts, were in his original Hebrew the conjunction ve (English and) ; and, as has been said (p. 28 n. 2, p. 50 n. 1), and in Hebraistic Greek does not necessarily imply chronological sequence. We have, however, distinguished the connectives then (τότε), which implies sequence, and while He was speaking these things (Matt. ix. 14, 18), which implies immediate sequence or accompaniment (p. 29, note). The expression 'at that season' (ἐν ἐκείνῳ τῷ καιρῷ, Matt. xi. 25 ; xii. 1) has a wide sense. It is to be noted that the rest promised to the weary and heavy laden in the last verses of Matt. xi. is connected in sense with the question of the Sabbath rest (Matt. xii.) which the words 'at that season' introduce. The expression 'at that season' certainly does not necessarily mean that the plucking of the ears of corn followed the discourse which Matthew connects with the message of John, but only that the events recorded in both chapters occurred in the same season. To define time more exactly St. Luke employs the expressions 'in that very hour' (Luke ii. 38 ; vii. 21 ; x. 21 ; xii. 12 ; xx. 19 ; xxiv. 13) and 'in that very day' (xiii. 31 ; xxiii. 12 ; xxiv. 13) ; but when on one occasion (Luke xiii. 1) he says 'at that season,' he is connecting statements about the judgment. The cautions to the disciples mentioned in Luke xvii. 1-4, and connected with what precedes by and (not then), are similar in substance to what St. Matthew's connectives at that hour and then (xviii. 1, 21) would lead us to suppose were spoken at Capernaum. But whether Christ repeated some of His lessons, or Luke transposed some of them, it need not be supposed that St. Luke disregards chronological sequence in relating such events as the Mission of the Seventy.

VI. In this, as in most harmonies, Jesus is represented as having finally arrived in Bethany on Friday afternoon, six exact days before the killing of the Paschal lambs on Thursday afternoon, and as having eaten the Passover on the night before He suffered. If our explanations of St. John's language be accepted, the alternative, which supposes St. John to mean that Christ was crucified when the Paschal lambs were being slain, will be set aside as a needless supposition of discrepancy. But, at all events, the arrangement of the Passion week does not affect that of the previous years.

CLASSIFICATION OF ALL THE ALLEGED GOSPEL DIVER-
GENCIES OR HARMONISTIC DIFFICULTIES ACCORDING
TO THE NATURE OF THEIR EXPLANATION.

(a) *Words are liable to ambiguity.*

(b) *Language has its legitimate range.*

(c) *Different evangelists select different details.*

(d) *Different events may be somewhat similar.*

1. The four fishermen were probably called before the miraculous draught of fishes, which was a significant prelude to the coming circuit, though the narratives might be combined . 28
2. The two visits to Nazareth must not be confounded, as they fittingly closed the first and second years' ministry, as Christ's appearance at the Feast of Dedication closed the third . . 21, 27
3. There were probably two anointings of Jesus 30, 50
4. Some Parables are similar, and some discourses were recapitulated

(e) *The order of the Gospels follows the ordinary rules.*

1. St. Matthew's order, in grouping precepts, miracles, and parables doctrinally, is sometimes not chronological . . 3
2. *And* does not always imply sequence ; *e.g.* the question mentioned in Luke xxi. 7 was asked not at the gate of the Temple but on the Mount of Olives . . . 28, *n.* [2], 50, *n.*
3. After mentioning the disciples' ambitious reasoning, St. Luke gives at once Christ's reproval, though this followed some time after at Capernaum . . . . 50, *n*
4. After mentioning the first inquiry of Bartimæus at the entrance to Jericho, St. Luke at once relates his cure, though it took place when Jesus left Jericho . . . . . 43, 49, *n.*
5. St. Matthew and St. Mark do not relate Christ's visit to Bethany, six days before the Passover, and, therefore, do not mention the anointing till afterwards . . . . . 50, *n.*

(f) *Undue deference must not be given to the exceptional ancient codices, the Vatican Codex* (B) *and the Sinaitic Codex* (ℵ). *Their aberrations are attributed by Abbé Martin to the misuse of Origen's writings, and to quotations made often from memory by the Fathers. Corrupt codices existed long before them* (*Eus.* v. 28).

1. In Mark i. 2 the reading 'prophets' is as well supported as 'Esaias' ; but, if we adopt the latter, see b 2
2. In Matt. x. 10 and Luke ix. 3 the reading 'staves' is as well supported as 'staff'; the rod (staff) here meant was, at all events, for tenting purposes, see a 5
3. In deference to B and ℵ, and in spite of nearly all other evidence, the Revisers have shortened the remarks of Jesus about the casting out of the deaf and dumb spirit of the epileptic boy ; but, if we adopt their readings, they may be combined. See c 11
4. On little better grounds, they have given a different answer in Matthew's account of the Rich Young Ruler ; but this answer might readily be combined with the other. See c 13
5. On even less grounds, they have adopted a reading in Luke xxiii. 45, which, if properly translated, would imply that there was an eclipse of the sun at the Passover, held at full moon . 54